Tradition and Sanity

BOOKS BY PETER KWASNIEWSKI

Resurgent in the Midst of Crisis: Sacred Liturgy,
the Traditional Latin Mass, and Renewal in the Church

Noble Beauty, Transcendent Holiness:
Why the Modern Age Needs the Mass of Ages

A Reader in Catholic Social Teaching:
From Syllabus Errorum *to* Deus Caritas Est

Sacred Choral Works

Peter A. Kwasniewski

Tradition and Sanity

*Conversations & Dialogues
of a Postconciliar Exile*

✝

✠ Angelico Press

First published
by Angelico Press © 2018

For information, address:
Angelico Press
169 Monitor St.
Brooklyn, NY 11222
www.angelicopress.com

978-1-62138-417-5 (pbk)
978-1-62138-418-2 (cloth)
978-1-62138-419-97 (ebook)

Cover design: Michael Schrauzer
Image credit: photograph by Dom Benedict Anderson, O.S.B.,
Monk of Silverstream Priory. Used with permission.

CONTENTS

Preface i

Acknowledgments vi

1 "An Awesome, Time-transcending, Cosmic Sacrifice" 1

2 At Loggerheads 19

3 "The Old Mass Never Deviates from the Gaze of the Lord" 27

4 On Liturgical Development and Corruption 43

5 "Where Angels Chant Before the Pierced and Glorified Lamb" 53

6 Why Catholics Are So Bad at Evangelizing—And What Needs to Change 63

7 "A Deeply Felt Hunger and Thirst for the Unequivocally Sacred" 75

8 The Papacy: In Service of Sacred Tradition 85

9 Gnosticism, Liturgical Change, and Catholic Life 99

10 May We Question the Liturgical Reform? 117

11 "The Glue that Holds All of Catholicism Together" 131

12 Recent Profane Novelties 141

13 "Long Before This Brigade of -isms Muscled In" 157

14 A Nightmare and a Dream 163

15 "Nostalgically Stuck in the Spirit of Vatican II" 169

16 A Day in the Life of a Monastery, Some Years in the Future 175

17 "It's Time We Stopped the Musical Starvation Diet" 183

18 In the Reign of Pope Leo XIV 207

*In gratitude for all traditional monks and nuns
who perpetuate in time and space the eternal chant of divine praise
and channel its divinizing rivers into our mortal drought*

Thine eyes shall see the king in his beauty: they shall behold a land of far distances.

Isaiah 33:17

You shall seek me, and you shall find me. Because you seek me with all your heart, I will let myself be found.

Into Great Silence

Gradually, as the sacred liturgy progressed, he became aware of a presence, intangible but real.... This reality pierced his insensibility, summoned him with insistence, demanded that he recognize it and give it a name. Something within him stirred and woke; he was in the midst of Beauty, and he knew it.

Michael Kent

Whoever lives the liturgical life of the Church according to her venerable and hallowed ordering will find therein all the grades of perfection; his life will become a work of beauty, and will attain its everlasting value in its progressive transfiguration.

Ildefons Herwegen, OSB

Number not thyself among the multitude of the disorderly.

Ecclesiasticus 7:17

Preface

The idea for this book first arose in exchanges I had with people around the world who told me that my interviews on Catholic liturgy, sacred music, the state of the Church, and the prospects for a revival of tradition were some of the most helpful treatments of these topics that they had seen. Such reactions encouraged me to think that the interviews might be of service to a larger audience if gathered into a book. Moreover, although my favorite genre is the essay, I had begun to write dialogues as well, some earnest and some humorous. Through them I sought to delve into thorny subjects in a more exploratory way. It occurred to me that these two sets of writings, the actual conversations and the fictional dialogues, paired well together.

What I say in the interviews comes straight out of my life experience as a Catholic "born out of season" (cf. 1 Cor 15:8), who, having been consigned to a lackluster childhood and adolescence in the postconciliar void, discovered in college the immense treasure of tradition. This discovery, which came with a shock of excitement and a strange sense of peril, turned everything upside-down or inside-out; my life would never be the same again. One might compare it to passing from two dimensions into three, or from a black-and-white world into a world of color. For the first time, Catholicism made sense to me as a total worldview in which everything found its proper place in a coherent whole: belief, work, leisure, art, science, beauty, suffering, love, worship, life, death, eternity.

What I write in the dialogues, on the other hand, derives more particularly from years of encounters with Catholics—laymen, religious, and clergy. My interlocutors fall into three categories: those who, like me, have fallen in love with tradition and are eager to go deeper; those who do not know tradition at all and yet, in their searching for beauty and for answers, are on the way to it; and those who, for a variety of reasons, some personal, some speculative, have rejected tradition or fight against it as a thing at odds with aggiornamental hygiene.

The book is meant as a point of departure, not a point of arrival—or better, as a way station, like those little shrines with a crucifix or an image of Our Lady that charm the countryside of Europe. For Christians are *in via* from baptism until they pass into eternity, pilgrims walking by the strength of divine food to that heavenly Jerusalem whose perfect worship we glimpse here in symbols and strain for in prayer. Traditional Catholicism, like the liturgy that is its crown jewel, is (as I call it) an "infinite expanse one never reaches the end of, to match the human soul's capacity for the infinite." As Pope Benedict XVI once said: "To go on pilgrimage is not simply to visit a place to admire its treasures of nature, art, or history. To go on pilgrimage really means to step out of ourselves in order to encounter God where He has revealed Himself, where His grace has shone with particular splendor and produced rich fruits of conversion and holiness among those who believe."[1] But is there any place where God has revealed Himself more frequently or more profoundly than in the universal shrine and everyday miracle of the Church's tradition—her traditional liturgy, devotions, spirituality, theology, way of life, her endlessly varied and colorful customs? In this sphere of peculiar favor, His grace has shone with a splendor unequaled by that of any other culture or civilization in the history of the world; from here, the richest fruits of holiness have taken their sap and burst forth. Above all, this sphere demands that we step out of ourselves, out of our fallen egoism and our temporal prejudices, into a new frame of reference that cleanses, challenges, compels us to the ground of humility before the Holy One.

> If you came this way,
> Taking any route, starting from anywhere,
> At any time or at any season,

1. Address of the Holy Father at the Cathedral of Santiago de Compostela, November 6, 2010.

It would always be the same: you would have to put off
Sense and notion. You are not here to verify,
Instruct yourself, or inform curiosity
Or carry report. You are here to kneel
Where prayer has been valid.[2]

We are always pilgrims *to* the haven of Catholic tradition: the treasure we are hunting, rejoicing in, sharing out with our fellows, is
not something we can ever fully possess or comprehend, much less
"master." We will always be inferior to it, smaller than it, indebted to
it, and pupils of it. We are drawn into its sphere of influence, step by
step, as we yield ourselves to the inexhaustible "inheritance of the
saints in light" (cf. Col 1:12).

After fifty years of utter devastation in the vineyard of the
Church, like the aftermath of a nuclear war in sheer scope of damage, we are in no position to say that we "have" our tradition, since
humanly speaking, we have lost hold of it, lost sight of it, lost the
enveloping natural givenness of it, and must labor in tears and in
the sweat of our brow to recover it piece by piece, rite by rite, chant
by chant, treatise by treatise, devotion by devotion—for all the
world like monks in the Dark Ages rebuilding a monastery for the
third or fourth time from the ruins left behind by the latest barbar-
ian horde. And of all wayward hordes, the techno-barbarians of
modernity are by far the worst, as having the worst philosophy and
the most material power. Nevertheless, can we not make the words
of Cardinal Ottaviani our own? "As horrendous and formidable as
they are, they do not frighten us. These new barbarians will also
pass, and perhaps the hour is at hand. The Church will not suc-
cumb."[3] Our struggle sets us not only "against principalities and
powers, against the rulers of the world of this darkness, against the
spirits of wickedness in the high places" (Eph 6:12), which is bad
enough, but also against these rulers' and spirits' earthly images and
effects: "pseudo-liturgical tomfoolery, communistic sloganeering,

---

2. T. S. Eliot, *Four Quartets*, "Little Gidding," ll. 39–46.
3. Trans. Francesca Romana, published at *Rorate Caeli* on June 16, 2015.

faithlessness thinly veiled with clerical verbiage, and total moral laxism (baptized as 'liberation')."[4]

Today, one can find an increasing number of "postconciliar exiles" who have learned that this haven of tradition exists. It is no fantasy, no castle in the air, no refuge for the world-weary, no *passepied* in mirror-lined halls of nostalgia. It is as real as—one may truthfully say, *more* real than—the eye that perceives it, the mind that knows it, the tongue that praises it; more real than the world graced by its visitation and confused by its absence. Its solidity and stability come from above, from the Father of lights, from the King of glory, from the celestial hierarchies, from the city of the living God. We have found our way to it through tortuous routes of conversion, yet we must work to keep it in view, as a captain heads his ship to port against contrary winds and waves. The haven exists, of that there can be no doubt—but we ourselves are not yet fully at home there, ensconced in our ancestral stronghold. One might almost address this participated likeness of God in the words of St Augustine's famous prayer: "You were with me, but I was not with you.... You called, you shouted, and you broke through my deafness. You flashed, you shone, and you dispelled my blindness. You breathed your fragrance on me; I drew in breath and now I pant for you. I have tasted you, now I hunger and thirst for more."[5]

May these conversations, real and imaginary, be a support to readers in thinking through and responding wisely to the challenges of a chaotic period in the history of the Catholic Church. "Not that we are sufficient to think anything of ourselves, as of ourselves: but our sufficiency is from God" (2 Cor 3:5). We will be saved by Him alone who says with divine right: "Fear not. I am the First and the Last, and alive, and was dead, and behold I am living for ever and ever, and have the keys of death and of hell" (Rev 1:17–18).

---

4. From Louis Bouyer's 1978 study of the Lefebvre case, "The Catholic Church in Crisis," trans. John Pepino, published at *Rorate Caeli* on July 6, 2015.

5. St Augustine, *Confessions*, Bk. 10, ch. 27.

O Oriens,
we have seen Thy light in the East,
rising at the high altar,
shining in the Holy Sacrifice,
radiant in all the rites of our religion,
and have come to adore Thee.
We have touched the hem of Thy garment
and found healing
from the hemorrhage of modernization,
the staunchless flow of empty promises,
of which no doctor could cure us
but Thou alone, O divine Physician.
Tu nobis, victor Rex, miserere.
Amen, alleluia.

SEPTEMBER 29, 2018
Dedication of St Michael the Archangel

Acknowledgments

The main title of this book pays playful homage to Frank Sheed's masterful *Theology and Sanity,* which every Catholic should read at one time or another. As in his day, the rapidly vanishing sanity of the Western world demanded the potent medicine of straight-up Thomism, so in our day, the rapidly vanishing sanity of the Catholic Church demands a resolute return to the fundamental sources of her identity, life, and mission.

The interview in chapter 1 was conducted in Norcia in July of 2017 by Hrvoje Juko and was published in English under the title "Interview with Dr Kwasniewski about Discovering the Old Mass, Progressive Liturgists, Common Objections, *Ad Orientem,* Optionitis, Antiquarianism, and More" at *Rorate Caeli* on November 3, 2017, and in Juko's Croatian translation "Moderni vijek i misa vjekova: prigovori i odgovori o tradicionalnoj liturgiji" at the website Bitno.net on October 29, 2017.

Chapter 2 appeared in the form of an epistolary exchange published at *OnePeterFive* on March 7, 2018, as "An Anti-Traditionalist Rants—and a Traditionalist Responds."

The interview in chapter 3 was conducted by Roseanne Sullivan and published as "Why Does the Modern Age Need the Mass of Ages?" in *The Latin Mass: The Journal of Catholic Culture and Tradition,* vol. 26, n. 4 (Christmas 2017): 46–51. Substantially the same interview also appeared online at *New Liturgical Movement* and *Homiletic & Pastoral Review.*

The dialogue in chapter 4 was first published at *New Liturgical Movement* on June 25, 2018, with the title "A Brief Dialogue on Liturgical Development and Corruption."

The interview in chapter 5 was coordinated for the Latin Mass Society of England & Wales by Sarah Whitebloom and appeared in a somewhat abridged form in *Mass of Ages,* n. 183 (Spring 2015), 4–6. The full version is included here.

Acknowledgments

The dialogue in chapter 6 was first published at *OnePeterFive* on November 22, 2017, with the title "Why Catholics Are So Bad at Evangelizing—And What Has to Change." The interview in chapter 7 was conducted by Andrej Kutarna of the publishing house Hesperion in Prague, as part of the run-up to the launch of the Czech edition of *Resurgent in the Midst of Crisis* (*Povstávání z prachu: Tradiční liturgie a obnova Církve*). A Czech translation of the interview, slightly abridged, appeared in the *Res Claritas Monitor* 13 (2016), n. 18, 11–14. The full Czech translation, "Na prvním místě je Bůh—rozhovor," is available at http://hesperion.cz.

The dialogue in chapter 8 was first published at *OnePeterFive* on December 13, 2017, with the title "A Dialogue Between Two Monks Concerning the Papacy."

Chapter 9 transcribes a panel discussion that took place in English as part of a study day held in Vienna on April 2, 2017 for the Austrian book launch of the German edition of *Resurgent in the Midst of Crisis* (*Neuanfang inmitten der Krise: Die heilige Liturgie, die traditionelle lateinische Messe und die Erneuerung in der Kirche*). The host was Wolfram Schrems, and the other two guests were Dr Thomas Stark and P. Edmund Waldstein, O.Cist. I am grateful for their permission to publish this transcript in the present book.

Chapter 10 first appeared at *OnePeterFive* on June 21, 2018, under the title "Are Faithful Catholics Allowed to Question the Liturgical Reform?—A Dialogue."

The interviews in chapters 11 and 13 were both conducted by Maestro Aurelio Porfiri, a writer for *O Clarim*, a publication of the Diocese of Macau. The first appeared in *O Clarim* in two parts: on September 23, 2016, with the title "Liturgy in the midst of crisis," and on September 30, 2016, with the title "Seeds of renewal." The second interview appeared in *O Clarim* on September 22, 2017, under the title "A Noble Beauty."

The dialogues in chapters 12, 14, 16, and 18 were published anonymously in *The Latin Mass: The Journal of Catholic Culture and Tradition*—the first as "Monks in Dialogue: Recent Profane Novelties," vol. 26, n. 4 (Christmas 2017): 74–79; the second as "A Nightmare and a Dream," vol. 25, n. 4 (Christmas 2016): 86–87; the third as "A

Day in the Life of a Monastery (Some Years in the Future)," vol. 26, n. 3 (Fall 2017): 76–79; the fourth as "In the Reign of Pope Leo XIV," vol. 27, n. 3 (Fall 2018): 78–79.

The interview in chapter 15 was conducted by Diane Montagna and published at *LifeSiteNews* on October 24, 2017, under the title "Pope's liturgy reforms risk taking Catholics 'back to the 1970s': liturgy expert." Diane also did a number of interviews with me on sacred music that I have shortened and combined to form Chapter 17. This material originally appeared at *Aleteia* in five separate installments: "Sacred music is alive and well" (August 22, 2016), "Human beings need beautiful things" (August 23, 2016), "How to bring better sacred music to your parish" (August 24, 2016), "Sacred music: Echoing on Earth the heavenly choir" (January 3, 2017), and "Church choirs: The good, the bad and the ugly" (January 4, 2017).

Characters and names in the dialogues are fictional; none is meant to represent any actual person.

All of the material has been edited to a greater or lesser extent for inclusion in this volume, principally to ensure a lack of redundancy. Footnotes have been added to indicate sources, but no effort has been made to provide a "scholarly apparatus," as that would be quite beside the point of a book like this. Readers who are seeking detailed references to sources and recommended further reading should consult my other two books published by Angelico, *Resurgent in the Midst of Crisis* and *Noble Beauty, Transcendent Holiness*, both of which furnish bibliographies.

I thank all the interviewers mentioned above for their initiative in approaching me and for the time they put into crafting excellent questions. I thank all the editors and publishers, whether paper-based or internet-based, whose support of my work has made it possible for me to devote myself full-time to the articulation and defense of traditional Catholicism. I particularly thank Angelico Press for doing such a fine job with my last two books on the liturgy that the question of who should publish the next one did not even arise in my mind. Lastly, I thank the three very special people who have endured much and given generously so that this, and all of my other work, could see the light of day.

1

"An Awesome, Time-transcending, Cosmic Sacrifice"

An Interview with Hrvoje Juko

Before we get into our questions today, Dr Kwasniewski, tell our readers about yourself. Where did you study and where do you teach?

I was born in Chicago, Illinois. I grew up in New Jersey, where I attended Catholic grade school and an all-boys high school run by Benedictine monks. During this time I sang in various parish and school choirs and started studying music. I went to Thomas Aquinas College in California for a bachelor's degree in liberal arts, then on to the Catholic University of America for a master's and a doctorate in philosophy, where I spent my time mostly in the study of Aristotle, Plato and the Platonists, and St Thomas Aquinas. I was hired by the International Theological Institute in Gaming, Austria, under the chancellorship of Cardinal Schönborn, and taught philosophy and theology there for almost 8 years. I left Austria to help establish a new liberal arts "Great Books" school in the United States called Wyoming Catholic College. Over the past decade, I've taught courses in philosophy, theology, art history, and music, and directed the choir and scholas for the liturgies.[1]

How did you get into the old Mass? Where did the interest arise from?

---

1. Dr Kwasniewski was a faculty member and choir director at Wyoming Catholic College from 2006–2018.

It happened somewhat gradually. I didn't grow up with it at all. I was born in 1971, so I just never saw it; I never even knew it existed, as is the case for a lot of people of my generation and younger. We're the people Pope Benedict XVI was talking about in his letter to the bishops of July 7, 2007, when he said that "after the Second Vatican Council it was presumed that requests for the use of the 1962 Missal would be limited to the older generation which had grown up with it, but in the meantime it has clearly been demonstrated that young persons too have discovered this liturgical form, felt its attraction and found in it a form of encounter with the Mystery of the Most Holy Eucharist, particularly suited to them." So that's what happened with me. I found out at the end of high school, when I was 17 or 18, that there was such a thing as the traditional Latin liturgy. I didn't have it anywhere nearby, or at least I wasn't able to find out where it was (those were pre-internet days), so it was still a kind of theoretical knowledge. But I was becoming much more interested in the Faith at that time. I was studying it more carefully, I was trying to live it more fully, and so, when I had the opportunity in college to start attending the traditional liturgy occasionally, it really spoke to me.

How did it strike you when you first started attending?

I found that there was a very deep sense of the mystery of the Mass, of the reverence that we owe to it. And the seriousness of the liturgy was something that really impressed me. Of course, we know that a Mass celebrated with the proper intention and the proper matter is a valid Mass, but in a lot of liturgies I had been to in my life, it seemed as if people weren't really serious about what they were doing. And when I went to the old Mass, there was this total focus on God and on our Lord Jesus Christ. It was something that both attracted me and provoked me, because it made me wonder: if we really believe what we say we believe about the Mass and the Eucharist, why shouldn't we *always* be treating it with this massive adoration and reverence, this devotion, care, and seriousness? Why shouldn't we do that?

That began a journey for me of several years, at the end of which

I was simply going whenever I could to the traditional liturgy, and only going to the new one when I had to or when I had the ability to influence for the better how it was celebrated, usually through leading sacred music.

The standard liturgical narrative from some professors is that, back before Vatican II, there were the Bad Old Days™. The liturgy was distant, incomprehensible to the faithful, almost conceived of as a magical ritual: the priest does his magical thing there, and the faithful were passive observers, as if they were attending a play or an opera. Basically, Granny prayed her Rosary, and that was the extent of her liturgical participation. And then came Vatican II, and the reforms after Vatican II. They did away with useless repetition and all of the medieval accretions and impurities that crept into the original, pure liturgy of the early Church. Vatican II insisted on vernacularization so that Mass could be understandable, and the altars were turned around so that people could understand what is happening and actively participate in what is going on. So we're living in the Good New Days™. But you don't buy this narrative, do you?

No, I don't. Of course you've raised a lot of different questions, so let me see if I can address several of them.

The first and most basic fact is that we will never understand the mystery of the sacred liturgy, we will never comprehend it, because it is from God and for God; indeed, it has the very presence of God within it. St Augustine says, "if you comprehend it, it's not God,"[2] and there should be something similar going on with the liturgy. Obviously we want to have *some* notion of what we're doing, what we're involved in, but the idea of making it all intelligible to people actually leads to a dumbing-down of the liturgy, where the prayers are put into everyday language, and the mystery evaporates—that is, the mystery of our participation in an awesome, time-transcending, cosmic sacrifice which is more important than anything else we do, and more mysterious than anything else we do; something that's really transcendent, that should leave us speechless, full of wonder.

2. "Si comprehendis, non est Deus" (*Sermon* 117).

The idea that we can somehow wrap this up in a package and hand it over to people, and say: "Okay, now you've got it, we're done with our work"—this is profoundly contrary to the nature of the liturgy. That's why we see, when we look at the history of liturgy in every period and in every place, there are always features of the liturgy that emphasize its solemnity, its sacredness, its specialness, the fact that this is something set apart from everyday life.

The Byzantine liturgy is full of this. And even though Byzantine liturgy can sometimes be in the language of the people, it features an iconostasis that separates the holy place from the congregation, there are many things that only the clergy can do, there are many silent prayers, there are copious signs of reverence and awe that show us that this is not the marketplace, this is not the business office, this is not the classroom—this is a special and sacred time. Liturgy needs to have elements in it that unmistakably convey that message to us.

One of them for the West was Latin. Once upon a time people spoke Latin, fair enough; but nobody spoke the Latin *of the liturgy*—that's a very formal, high, polished, elegant, eloquent Latin, poetic Latin. As time went on, the Latin language became a kind of badge of the distinctiveness of the liturgy: this is the only place where you encounter these prayers said in these ways. Eventually that became, I would argue, a kind of sacramental, like holy water or like the Rosary; it became something that led us to holiness. Even though in and of itself Latin is just a language, the Latin of the liturgy became a hallowed vehicle for connecting us with the divine.

The other thing I want to say in connection with this is that liturgists in the 50's, 60's, and 70's were often guilty of a kind of contempt for common people. They spoke of the common people as though they had no understanding—they were just so ignorant, and illiterate, and unwashed, and disgraceful... and we intelligent, expert liturgists, *we* have to *retrain* them and show them what it really means to be Christian. That's an incredible arrogance. The Catholic faith flourished for centuries and centuries with people who supposedly "didn't understand the liturgy," and now, with all the expert advice—is it flourishing? I don't think it is. You can't necessarily blame that only on the liturgical reform, but in any case what they predicted didn't happen—in fact, the opposite happened. So whether that's a cause or a coincidence, we certainly can't exalt the new liturgy as a great success.

There's that famous story that the Curé of Ars found an old man in his church who was just sitting there for long periods of time, and the curé finally asked him one day: "What are you doing?" And he said: "I look at him, and He looks at me." And the *Catechism* quotes this as a perfect expression of contemplative prayer, the essence of prayer.[3] That's the kind of prayer that people encounter with the old liturgy, and that's what Granny was doing more often than not—not just mindlessly telling her beads. I think we need to recognize and recapture the profound piety that people had, which was nourished by the liturgy.

There are several other things you asked about—do you want to go over them one by one?

I'll just throw out the more or less standard objections you can hear, and give you the opportunity to respond. One objection would be something like this: Vatican II called for active participation. But you can't participate actively unless you understand the prayers or the readings or what's going on. So we need vernacular liturgy.

Right, that's what they say. The problem is, active participation—as defined by Vatican II, no less[4]—is primarily the investment of the mind and the heart in what is going on. So the first thing presupposed in active participation is that you have a correct notion of what the Mass is, what the liturgy is: that it's the holy sacrifice of the Cross, your participation in the redemptive Passion of our Lord, and in all the mysteries of His life. So, if you don't have that understanding, if the liturgy doesn't nourish that deep understanding in the mind, and in the heart, then it does not matter how much

---

3. See *Catechism of the Catholic Church*, n. 2715.

4. The Constitution on the Sacred Liturgy *Sacrosanctum Concilium* (December 4, 1963) always places the term "internal" before the term "external": see nn. 17–19, n. 99, and n. 110. In this way it implies that the relationship is like that of soul to body, the one functioning as formal, efficient, and final cause, the other as material cause.

you're standing up, sitting down, kneeling, speaking, singing, clapping. It doesn't matter what you're doing actively, externally, if you don't have that interior participation in the Mass.

What we've seen, anyway, is a transition from a Catholic world in which participation was real but mostly silent and interior to a world in which participation is external and vocal but without a lot of actual *understanding*, without being in sync with "the spirit of the liturgy" as Guardini and Ratzinger talk about it.[5]

External participation does have a place, and yet, it's not the most important place. Without a doubt, there have been times and places where people could have been more involved in the liturgy, they could have had a better understanding of its prayers, they could have sung the Gregorian chants of the Ordinary as Pope Pius X asked for—Pius XI, Pius XII, many popes asked for that. It's clear that we need to have *both* interior and exterior participation, and that both of these constitute active participation. There's a real danger in a simplistic understanding of "active."

Sometimes it's mentioned that maybe a better translation of the term "active participation" would be "actual participation," since the Latin term actuosa *means actual, not activity in the sense of "I'm doing all these things."*

Yes, I think that's true. It means fully engaged, with all of one's powers.

How about this: the original language of the Roman rite was Greek, and it only got translated into Latin when people no longer understood Greek. So, what the reformers did in our times was basically the same. Out of pastoral concern, they made the liturgy understandable, or at least more accessible to the people. Why would we want something most people can't understand?

That's an interesting question. The early Church prayed in Greek.

5. Namely, in the book written by each under the same title: *The Spirit of the Liturgy.*

That wasn't the common language of everybody, but it was a widespread language, and it was also the language of the intelligentsia, so the liturgy was able to be conducted in a formal manner in that language. It seems that the Church, always acting from a deep conservatism, hesitated for quite a while before making the switch from Greek to Latin—that is, the Church in Rome, the Western Church, so to speak. And when that change was made, the kind of Latin into which the liturgy was translated was, as I said before, a noble and high version of the Latin language. It wasn't the street language; it wasn't the vernacular, the everyday speech.

But the interesting thing is that having made that shift, that fundamental shift, it seems that the Church never—never until the end of the twentieth century—seriously called it into question. We have to respect the fact that the pace of change in liturgical history slows down as we go through the centuries. Things are added, but what's already there is preserved. As Catholics we believe that the Holy Spirit guides the development of the liturgy, its organic development. So, had it truly been necessary or even advisable for the Church to switch from Latin into other languages, she would have done that, and much earlier on, too. The fact that she *didn't* do that even after other languages had developed out of Latin (especially the Romance languages), and even when the missionaries brought the Latin liturgy to the New World, and to the Far East, and to tribes in Africa that had no clue about Latin—the fact that the Church held firmly to that Latin liturgical heritage meant that it had become something far more than a practical convention to her. It had become something sacred, something precious, something extremely valuable that wasn't a mere external; it wasn't just like the color of someone's hair or eyes, or the fashion of their clothing.

Here is a good comparison: the vestments of the liturgy. As you know, these vestments are adaptations of ancient Roman clothing, common Roman clothing. But after a certain point, the development of the liturgical clothing stopped. Meanwhile secular clothing kept developing, and a hundred different styles of clothing have come and gone, but the liturgical clothing—while it developed a little bit; there are different types, different cuts, different styles—it's fundamentally the same as ever: you always have the alb, and the chasuble, and the amice, and the maniple, even though they might take on different shapes or colors. In liturgical history you have more development earlier on, and less development later on. This, it seems to me, makes sense, because as the liturgy is brought to greater and greater fullness and perfection, it shouldn't need to change much anymore, nor would ordinary Christians want to see it change. It is a splendid, rambling, comfortable old home in which they are happy to live.

The funny thing to me is that we didn't have serious complaints about the Latin liturgy from anyone but the experts. It's the self-styled experts who kept saying: "Oh no, we have to change this for the common people." The common people weren't out there clamoring, and signing petitions or marching with placards saying: "We need the liturgy in Italian, or Spanish, or French, or German." They liked the fact that it was always the same, and wherever you went, you found the same liturgy.

Maybe a relevant point would be that the actual conciliar text about liturgical reform, Sacrosanctum Concilium, *said that Latin should be retained, not abolished.*

Exactly. It said that the limits of the vernacular could be extended; the use of it could be extended, but it went on to say that it would make the most sense to extend it only to the parts of the Mass that are changing from day to day.[6]

So, another way of thinking about your question: most of the liturgy of the Church is stable and repetitious. You only have to hear the Kyrie or the Gloria a few times before you can figure out what it's saying. I know from experience that my children, and the children of many other families in the communities I've lived in, can sing, and recite, and understand the repeated Latin prayers of the liturgy.

Again, I think this goes back to contempt for the intelligence of ordinary Catholics. The liturgy of the Mass can be printed on a few pages—it's not a lot of text. And beyond that, of course, we have the

6. See *Sacrosanctum Concilium*, nn. 36, 54, 91, 101.

fact that as time goes on, we also have an increase in literacy. Part of the Liturgical Movement in its healthy phase was reintroducing people to the prayers of the liturgy through printed missals. By the time you get to the middle of the twentieth century, anybody who can read can follow the entire liturgy from start to finish—they don't *need* to do that every single occasion, but they're capable of doing that, and they often did exactly that. Really, it's more about educating people in the riches of their own heritage than about changing it all around on the assumption that they aren't educated or won't ever get educated. That seems like a defeatist attitude.

Do you think the exodus of the faithful from the mid-60's to the mid-70's had to do with the liturgical reform?

It had a lot of cultural causes, including the sexual revolution, but there's no question that the number, magnitude, and rapidity of the changes to the liturgy played a huge part in disorienting, disenchanting, and disinheriting the Catholic faithful from their own Church. It was as if the clergy were suddenly springing a new religion on them, with new "values" and new "priorities." Some adapted to it willingly, some went along with it grudgingly, and all too many marched right out the doors, never to return. Bill Buckley, a famous American political journalist, said he wanted to believe that the changes handed down from the hierarchy must somehow be for the good of the people, but he said it was the hardest act of faith he'd ever had to make—and the fruits of it were never apparent.[7]

One might almost think of it as reverse transubstantiation: we had the living body of Catholic tradition with all its beauty and nobility, and now the Church was transforming it back into ordi-

---

7. In an article published in *Commonweal* on November 10, 1967—therefore *prior* to the imposition of the Novus Ordo Missae, at a time when the old liturgy was still being used, albeit in a mangled vernacular form—William F. Buckley Jr. wrote: "I pray the sacrifice [of tradition and beauty] will yield a rich harvest of informed Christians. But to suppose that it will is the most difficult act of faith I have ever been called upon to make, because it tears against the perceptions of all my senses. My faith is a congeries of dogmatical certitudes, one of which is that the new liturgy is the triumph, yea the Resurrection, of the Philistines."

nary bread. But in our hearts we want the living body. The world is full of bread and gives it out plentifully to those who serve its interests. The Church is meant to give us what the world cannot. In the end, I guess I'm just elaborating on Ratzinger's sober statement: "The crisis in the Church is to a large extent caused by the crisis in the liturgy."[8]

Cardinal Sarah has been saying similar things about the controversial topic of liturgical orientation. One argument you hear for celebrating Mass versus populum (towards the people) is that the laity should join themselves to the sacrifice of the Mass, but they also have a royal priestly character, besides the ministerial priesthood of the priest. So, they have the right to see what's going on at the altar, and that means versus populum is the better option.

That's a very weak argument. The faithful don't have a "right" to see what's going on at the altar because, in a sense, there's nothing to see. The miracle of transubstantiation isn't visible, and, as William Mahrt pointed out, when the priest turned around, and people could see what he was doing, suddenly they didn't think it was such a big deal anymore. Because, in reality, the Mass is addressed to our *faith*, not to our sight. It's not about watching a show—let's say, a cooking demonstration going on in front of you, where you put in a little bit of this spice, and that herb, and you learn how to mix it up yourself. Well, you're never going to confect this mystery unless you're a priest, so you don't need to "see it."

The deeper issue here is that when the priest faces eastwards, he is facing in the same direction as the people. Or rather, the people are facing in the same direction as the priest. And it's clearer that *everyone* is offering the sacrifice—the priest in his own priestly way, and the people in their baptismal way, with their baptismal priesthood. Everybody is united in offering up the sacrifice of praise to the

8. The exact quotation from *Milestones: Memoirs 1927–1977*, trans. Erasmo Leiva-Merikakis (San Francisco: Ignatius Press, 1998): "I am convinced that the crisis in the Church that we are experiencing today is, to a large extent, due to the disintegration of the liturgy" (148).

East—and Scripture says that the East is a symbol of Christ who is to come, and He will come to us from the East. That eschatological sign is the sign of our longing for heaven, and for the return of Christ. As it says in the Book of Revelation, *maranatha*, "come, Lord Jesus." That whole symbolism, in my experience, makes people feel *more* involved in the offering of the Mass, rather than less involved.

If the priest turns around and is facing the people, suddenly there's a dynamic of the priest and the people who are facing off to each other, and now the priest is over against the people as somebody who has to entertain them or animate them or get their attention or be careful how his hair looks or how his face looks. Suddenly there's this dichotomy, maybe even an antagonism between the two parties, whereas when the priest turns around, he becomes anonymous, he is the icon of Christ, and all the people can, so to speak, "ride up to heaven" on his chasuble. I think that's exactly the experience people have at a Mass celebrated *ad orientem.*

When people go to Mass, and they see the priest not facing them, maybe it's uncomfortable for them at first, but it helps them to realize that this is not about *us.* The priest is not talking to us; he's talking to God. The priest is offering a sacrifice to God, from which we benefit. And therefore it's very important for us not to have the Mass turned towards us—that's a fundamental error, that's what we call anthropocentrism.

Wasn't it Ratzinger who said that the priest is not "turning his back to the people," it's more like he's leading them?

Exactly. As it's been humorously said, would you want the pilot of your airplane to be facing you or facing forward? Whenever you're going somewhere, everybody should be facing in the same direction. No one walks on a pilgrimage route backwards.

It's often said to "reform of the reform" types and traditionalists: "You people insist on organic development. You object to construction by committee. But what Trent did was not organic development; it did exactly the same thing as the reformers after Vatican II: to the best of its abilities, it got some experts, and they tried to restore the liturgy of the Fathers. And then it imposed this rite, which was the result of the work of experts."

This is a fallacious argument. Anybody who has studied liturgical history knows that the reforms that took place after the council of Trent were minor reforms compared to the ones that took place in the mid-to-late 1960s. For example, the order of Mass contained in the missal of Pius V, promulgated in 1570, is fundamentally the same as what you find in Rome in the fifteenth century, which is the same as what you find in the fourteenth century—and you can keep going back. The very heart of the Mass, the Roman Canon, goes all the way back to the sixth century and earlier, but its definitive form is already given to us from the late sixth century. The changes made in the Tridentine period under Pius V were ones that anybody would recognize as cosmetic, minor changes.

Maybe the biggest change made in the Tridentine missal was the abolition of most of the Sequences. And there are people today who regret that fact, but what Pius V's committee saw was that of all of the parts of the Mass, those were the most recent additions. They were also the most regionally diversified, and of uneven quality. In order to preserve what everybody had preserved up until that time, they thought that a simplification of the Sequences was advisable. One could agree or disagree, but it's interesting to me that that was the only major target or casualty, you might say, of that commit-tee—something that had developed rather recently, not the things that had been in place for centuries. *Those* are the things they would have never dreamed of taking away.

Moreover, bear in mind that Pius V's edition of the missal *added* certain things to the order of Mass. For example, the prayers at the foot of the altar—which are beloved to Catholics who attend the old Mass all over the world (Psalm 42, the double *Confiteor*, the dia-logue, the prayers going up to the altar)—those things started as private priestly prayers of preparation, but Pius V ordered that they be included in the order of the Mass. And that was an *enrichment* of the Mass, that wasn't changing something, or subtracting some-thing, but adding something. That's generally the way liturgical his-tory works—by addition, not by subtraction. Similarly, the last

Gospel became fused with the liturgy, when before it had been a private devotion of the priest, an act of thanksgiving. After 1570, everyone got to make that act and time of thanksgiving their own. We have to distinguish between liturgical change that consists in enhancement or addition, and liturgical change that consists in diminishment, or even destruction.

On the topic of enhancement, couldn't someone say: The new Mass introduced many, many options, even many new canons—including Eucharistic Prayers for Masses with Children and things like that. So, if liturgy develops by way of addition, we've got a whole bunch of new options. Isn't that good?

No, no, options are terrible. They lead to the disease I call "option-itis." In all traditional liturgies of East and West, no matter which one you look at—whether it's the Mozarabic, or the Syro-Malabar, or the Byzantine, or the Ambrosian, or the Roman, whatever tradition you look at—there's a certain point after which (and it's pretty early on, it's in the first millennium for sure, and even the first half of the first millennium) you have fixity of liturgical forms developing, whereby priests and bishops inherit a certain body of prayers and texts and chants and readings, and those are the ones they use. They don't tamper with them; they perpetuate them. Whatever was happening in the early centuries—and we have very scattered and incomplete records of that period—it's nevertheless a fact that there was an inherent drive in Christianity towards fixity of liturgical forms. And this is not some kind of late medieval corruption, it was something you see early on—you see it in Pope Gregory the Great, who died in 604. So this is very early indeed. Pope Gregory the Great is already finalizing various prayers so that they can have that nobility and fixity of form.

The reason for this, it seems to me, is quite simple: when you're dealing with the most sacred and solemn realities of all, you want to use the most noble, beautiful, orthodox, well-expressed prayers. And if you've inherited them, why would you think that you're better than your ancestors; that you could invent a better prayer, or that you could spontaneously do something better? In fact, when most people have to make up something extemporaneously, it's a bit of an embarrassment. You see this at weddings, when people have to make toasts. If they could memorize a famous toast, they'd probably end up doing a lot better than if they just tried to make one up themselves. And this is just a toast, which has no lasting significance. But when we're talking about the awesome sacrifice of the Mass, or baptism, or confirmation, or penance, or any of the sacraments, there's a reason why the Christian people has this instinct for preservation and conservation, fixity and stability.

What the modern options have done to the liturgy, and especially the openings for the priest to make things up in his own words, to use "these or similar words," what it's actually led to is a lot of banality in the liturgy, a lot of sub-standard, second-rate pseudo-liturgy. And you never know what you're going to get, that's the problem. It's like going to McDonald's or Burger King—are you going to get this option, or this option, or this option? In that sense it's very disconcerting for the faithful, who just want to get out of the noisy confusion of the secular world and focus as purely as they can on the Lord, and really give that time of prayer to Him. If you're going in and things are always changing, like a ground that's shifting underneath you, it's very difficult to establish that relationship of prayer. It's just a profoundly unsettling aspect of the new liturgy.

Given all the various options that are liturgically lawful in the missal of Pope Paul VI, you can celebrate the new Mass in a way that would be, to an outside observer, practically indistinguishable from the old Mass—ad orientem, *using exclusively Latin, chanting the readings, etc.—but you can also celebrate it in a completely different way that emphasizes the differences between what we now call the two forms.*

That's true. As Martin Mosebach says: "It is possible to celebrate the new Mass reverently and beautifully—but that is precisely the problem."[9] In other words, it should be *necessary* to do it that way. And

---

9. The exact quotation from *The Heresy of Formlessness: The Roman Liturgy and Its Enemy*, revised and expanded edition (Brooklyn: Angelico Press, 2018), 15–16: "Many people, too, concerned about these issues, will ask, 'Isn't it still possible to

that's the way it is with the old liturgy: if you follow the rubrics, it will be done properly; it will be done suitably, and fittingly. With the new Mass the priest has to be a holy person. Now, of course, the priest should always be a holy person, but with the new Mass, if he's not holy, then the liturgy could be a disaster, whereas if he is holy, he will do something that is prayerful and reverent. One could apply to the old Mass the saying about an aircraft carrier: it's a machine built by geniuses so that it can be operated by idiots. That is to say, it has to be in a certain sense bomb-proof. You can't make it *rely* on the personality or holiness of the celebrant. This is to hold the entire congregation hostage to the good or bad qualities of an individual.

Let me pose a final argument to you. Benedict XVI famously said that what is held sacred by one generation cannot suddenly be considered dangerous and wholly disregarded. But the new Mass restored many of the things that the ancients held as sacred in their liturgies, such as prayers of the faithful, or the offertory procession—the procession with the gifts—or communion in the hand. So these shouldn't be considered dangerous and discarded today.

That's what people call a sophistical argument. There are two different levels on which one could answer that kind of argument. One level is simply to note, as Pius XII did in his encyclical *Mediator Dei* from 1947,[10] that just because certain things were done in the ancient Church, and have fallen out of practice for many centuries, doesn't automatically mean that you should reintroduce them right now. In fact, the Church deepens, grows in her understanding of the liturgy and of what she's doing. That's why we have liturgical development to begin with.

In the ancient Church, if people received in the hand—and, by the way, there's some scholarly debate over how widespread that

celebrate the new liturgy of Pope Paul VI worthily and reverently?' Naturally it is possible, but the very fact that *it is possible* is the weightiest argument against the new liturgy."

10. See nn. 59–64.

custom was, and even how to interpret certain Patristic texts on it—they received in the hand very reverently, they covered their hands with a cloth, and many precautions were taken so that none of the bread would be lost—precautions we don't take anymore; quite the contrary. So, we've revived in a fake way something that was done differently in the ancient Church. But more to the point, the reason that practice stopped is because at a certain point people realized: "You know, this isn't really working very well. Let's go to a system that works better." And so, we actually had a better way, a more reverent and correct way, of distributing communion, as even Paul VI recognized in *Memoriale Domini* of 1969, and the invoking of archaic practices is a smokescreen for the agenda of the liberals, which is to revise entirely the Catholic understanding of the Holy Eucharist.

So, I regret to say that there's a lot of... what shall I say... deception involved in making those kinds of arguments. People want to "go back to early practices" not because they are full of warm piety for the ancients (you can see that from how they turn a blind eye to the ascetical practices of the ancients, and their moral rigor!), but because the underdeveloped pluralism of early practices easily serves as a matrix for their modernist agendas—like the agenda of denying the Real Presence, or placing it on the same level as Christ's presence in the "gathered assembly."

The other kind of response to this argument is to recognize the inherent limits of "scholarship." Sometimes scholars or experts say that something was done in the ancient Church, reconstructing it based on bits of fragmentary evidence—but then later scholars come along and prove them wrong. In the early Latin tradition there wasn't an offertory procession like the kind of thing we have now, where a couple of people bring bread and wine down the aisle and give it to the priest, and he takes it up to the altar. There's very little evidence that anything like that ever took place in the Western liturgies. On the other hand, ironically, there was always some kind of offertory *rite*, yet this is just what Bugnini and the Consilium took out of the liturgy when they "reformed" it. The way it's done in the Novus Ordo, with the *faux* Jewish blessing, corresponds to nothing that was ever done historically in the Christian liturgy. And so it's a kind of artificial archeologism—it's not even a real recovery of something.

How about the prayer of the faithful?

The same thing: it's a theory you find in people like Josef Jungmann, that when the priest says "Oremus" at the beginning of the offertory, that's a leftover introduction to the prayer of the faithful.[11] But there are other good scholars who say, "No, that's not at all what that was for," and that the prayers we find on Good Friday—those long intercessions—were for special occasions, they weren't an everyday or even every-Sunday affair. (We're speaking about the Roman rite and its close relatives. The Ambrosian rite has wonderful intercessions akin to those of the Byzantine liturgy.) Apart, then, from being careful not to ignore how the Holy Spirit guides the Church and inspires the development of the liturgy, one also has to be suspicious about scholarly theories because the scholarly theories are often proved wrong.

There were scholars who argued that *versus populum* was the original format of the liturgy. But almost nobody holds that anymore. Scholars hold all kinds of positions, but not that one. Or that the Second Eucharistic Prayer of the Novus Ordo reflects a real ancient Roman anaphora composed by St Hippolytus, which was a view taken for granted in the middle of the twentieth century but now is by no means agreed upon. It's a dangerous thing to yoke yourself to a cart that's being driven by scholars, because they might just drive you off somewhere over a cliff. But if you connect yourself to tradition, you are guaranteed to be following in the line that the Holy Spirit willed for the Church.

On a final note, you wrote a couple of books on the liturgy, right? Tell us about those.

---

11. See Josef A. Jungmann, SJ, *The Mass of the Roman Rite: Its Origins and Development*, trans. Francis A. Brunner, CSSR (New York: Benzinger, 1955; rep. Notre Dame, IN: Christian Classics, 2012), vol. 1, 480–90.

Three years ago [2014] I published a book called *Resurgent in the Midst of Crisis*. The subtitle is "Sacred Liturgy, the Traditional Latin Mass, and Renewal in the Church." It's a number of essays that deal with important aspects of the liturgy. I aim to show people what's at stake in these questions. There's a lot at stake. For example, one chapter is about why it was such a bad idea to give up on private celebrations of the Mass in favor of concelebration. Another chapter is called "Latin: the Ideal Liturgical Language," where I make a case that Latin is not just a quaint tradition of the past but something vitally important for the unity, the self-identity, of the Catholic Church in the postmodern pluralistic world. This book, I'm happy to say, has been published in Czech, Polish, German, and Portuguese, with editions underway in Spanish, Italian, and Belarusian. It seems to have "struck a nerve."

The more recent book came out this past summer [2017]: *Noble Beauty, Transcendent Holiness: Why the Modern Age Needs the Mass of Ages*. I would describe it as a high-level apologetic for the recovery of traditional liturgy for modern and postmodern people—that is, assuming for the sake of argument that the traditional liturgy rightfully had a central place in the past, I want to make the argument that it is especially important for people *now*—that it responds to our particular needs now more than ever. And that, of course, sounds paradoxical, because people might think: "How can an elaborate medieval liturgy respond to the needs of man in the twenty-first century?" But I make that very argument at length: our problems, what we're lacking, what we're missing, what we're confused about, these are the things the traditional liturgy responds to in ways the new liturgy doesn't. The new liturgy confirms or supports us in some of our modern errors and modern misconceptions; it does not help us to dispel our spiritual malaise. *La messe de toujours*, "the Mass of always," provokes us and challenges us in ways that we need.

2

At Loggerheads

A brusque lady sporting rimless octagonal spectacles, her lips pursed and her purse swinging, walks up to the unsuspecting author at the coffee hour after Mass, and accosts him without prefatory pleasantries. The author knows just who it is and smiles weakly as he readies himself for a demanding conversation.

Lady: If you want to recycle the claim, admittedly put about by Cardinal Ratzinger, that the new Mass was created by a committee, then you need to think through what he meant. *All* rites of Mass, in the end, have to pass through committees in Rome before they get an approbation!

Author: I'm afraid I can't agree with what you're saying. There were no committees in the early Church, nor in the "Dark Ages," nor in the High Middle Ages. The origins of our worship are hidden in their apostolic beginnings, from which we derive all the great families of rites, each with its own organic expansion and articulation as the centuries pass. The content grows now with this addition, now with that, often made by saintly individuals or anonymous monks inspired to contribute a new beauty to the common endeavor, which they would never dare to redesign, much less suppress. The liturgy reaches us by being handed down with veneration and received with trepidation.

Lady: So you admit that there is change, and that individuals make contributions? If that's the case, I don't see why you should have any problem with a committee—after all, it's just a bunch of individuals, presumably well-motivated, working for the good of the Church.

Author: Of course I admit there's change. No traditionalist thinks that the liturgy was handed down from heaven in its full splendor on the day of Pentecost. It can be and was meant to be elaborated, augmented, and refined, and very occasionally pruned. But it has never been a committee product. A committee *advised* St Pius V, but the missal he promulgated was, in all essentials, that which the church in Rome had long been celebrating. Sequences were removed and the calendar was simplified. This is like a gardener clipping off a few branches of an already mature tree.

Lady: That's a lovely metaphor, but what about the gardener who unearths old treasures that were buried and forgotten? If you read Bugnini,[1] whom you did not mention in your last book, or Lauren Pristas, who has published extensively on the orations and proves they were brought out of the riches of the old liturgies, not created out of thin air, the claim can no longer be seriously maintained that the Church produced a "botched" rite.

Author: Look, what happened in the 1960's under the Consilium had absolutely no historical precedent in either its scope or its outcomes. Anyone who has studied the history of the liturgy seriously cannot dispute this point. The very same Dr Pristas herself establishes it in her book on the Collects.[2] Who cares if the revisers plied their scissors and paste on old liturgical codices? What they did was artificial and egotistical. They had no trust or love for the inherited rites. It's as if the gardener cut down half the tree, spliced in several other species of trees, injected genetically modified cells, and painted the trunk a different color.

Lady: How recklessly you indulge in metaphors!

---

1. Annibale Bugnini, *The Reform of the Liturgy, 1948–1975*, trans. Matthew J. O'Connell (Collegeville, MN: The Liturgical Press, 1990).
2. Lauren Pristas, *The Collects of the Roman Missals: A Comparative Study of the Sundays in Proper Seasons before and after the Second Vatican Council* (London/New York: Bloomsbury T&T Clark, 2013).

Author: Let me try to say this more philosophically, then. The crisis in the liturgy is caused by an Enlightenment rejection of the inherent authority of tradition over our minds. *We* want to be the creators and judges of tradition, which we are not and never will be. We can either humbly and gratefully receive it, or arrogantly assert control and mastery over it. Our attitude must be either Aquinas's or Descartes's. Even the reform-minded Louis Bouyer came to see this point before his death, and regretted the devastation that had been wrought in the name of "pastoral liturgy." In his *Memoirs*, he refers to the Consilium's work as "the *abortus* we brought forth."[3]

Lady: The liturgy reflected the turmoil in the world in 1968. Things have changed since then. The liturgy has settled down. I am an example of someone who fell in love with the old rite in 1997 but finds prayerful Catholics, prayerful priests, and devout liturgies throughout the world as I travel. Your caricature of the Novus Ordo cannot be found in churches in the real world. It is part of a mythology in the service of quasi-schism.

Author: You speak of the liturgy as having "settled down." This it has done, for sure—into a routine of mediocrity, banality, and superficiality. If you have only ever found devout people led by priests who reverently celebrate the sacred mysteries, your travels have been fortunate indeed! Perhaps you need to travel some more in the United States, South America, and other places where liturgical abuses have become institutionalized, and clergy are persecuted if they challenge the status quo.

Lady: You refuse to acknowledge that there are many places where the new liturgy is done well.

Author: Of course the Novus Ordo can be celebrated "well," in a hermeneutic of continuity: one might think of the Oratory in Lon-

---

3. *The Memoirs of Louis Bouyer: From Youth and Conversion to Vatican II, the Liturgical Reform, and After*, trans. John Pepino (Kettering, OH: Angelico Press, 2015), 224.

don or in Oxford. But an approach that is completely faithful even to Vatican II's *Sacrosanctum Concilium* is as rare as an error-free airplane interview with Pope Francis.

Lady: You *had* to bring him into this...

Author: Besides, the problems with the Novus Ordo go much deeper than that. The reason it gets abused on a daily basis is that it was designed for ritual flexibility, cultural adaptation, pastoral accommodation. You can see this everywhere in its rubrics. It was, in that sense, doomed to abuse at the hands of people who lack the wisdom to submit to a tradition and the humility to deny themselves before the Holy—the sort of virtues inculcated by all traditional liturgical rites. The Novus Ordo is definitely *novus*; I'm just not sure it deserves to be dignified with the word *ordo*, for good order is perhaps its most notable shortcoming.

Lady: You recycle old canards instead of submitting them to critical scrutiny.

Author: It seems odd to speak of recycling old canards when my position, like that of many who came before me—Michael Davies, Klaus Gamber, László Dobszay—is based on a close study of the violence visited upon the Roman liturgy by self-styled reformers in the grip of ideologies that prejudiced them against nearly everything medieval and Baroque. Evidently they did not agree with Pope Pius XII that the slow development of the Church's liturgy over time is one of the ways in which the Holy Spirit leads the Church "into the fullness of truth," as Jesus promised.[4]

Lady: Did the Holy Spirit stop leading the Church in 1965 or so? The problem is not the Mass; the problem is poorly educated Catholics, out of their depth about their duties. We need arguments about truth, the nature of God, why Christ loves us... Stealing people for your minority pressure groups may, in some cases, be a way for-

---

4. See Encyclical Letter *Mediator Dei* (November 20, 1947), nn. 59–64.

ward, but you err wholly in believing that the old rite alone can accomplish the real work of Christianity, which is setting a good example everywhere I go. That, too, was what the Council wanted: a renewal of charity.

Author: Isn't it a problem of charity towards God and neighbor when the liturgy is abused? When it is turned into a means for celebrating the community? Or when it displays and transmits false doctrine? Did the Council want that?

Lady: Whatever else may be the case, I am sure that the Council didn't want Catholics only operating in enclaves where everybody agrees with one another! The point is to move on and move out to the streets where the problems are.

Author: You're sounding more and more like a certain dictator from South America.

Lady: Whether you're willing to admit it or not, Pope Francis has moved the conversation forward. It's all about *works*—who is an authentic Christian in the sacrifices they make for others! The reason why non-Christians or lapsed Christians love this pope is because they know he is getting at the heart of the Gospel. He comes to the aid of people in need.

Author (hesitates): Ah well, in addition to whatever good qualities he may have, Pope Francis has brought confusion and anguish, too. Whether he intends it or not, he has been undermining much of the good accomplished by John Paul II and Benedict XVI. It goes without saying that I pray for him every day, as every Catholic should. In fact, at parishes of the Institute of Christ the King, they add orations for the Holy Father at practically every Mass. I once suggested to a canon that the Institute should consider substituting the orations "Against the Persecutors of the Church," but this proposal didn't go over very well.

Lady: Do you think your pugnacity is helpful? I find it appalling.

Author: In a time of crisis, I say let there be a good fight, as there was during the early Christological and Trinitarian controversies, in the iconoclasm crisis, at the time of the Reformation, or in the early twentieth century against Modernism. Indifference, lukewarmness, and false peace are the bane of the Church in every age... but especially ours.

Lady: You keep speaking as if everything is in shambles. You bracket out the fact that many of the new movements, like Emmanuel—movements in every country of the world, and much more full of young people than the old rite Masses I attend—have contemporary music for their Masses. These services are prayerful, moving, and appealing to the next generation, with far more serious numbers than the old rite can boast. One does not have to have Gregorian chant to be transported. Your definition of beauty is too narrow. Your definition of tradition is too narrow. The Church is always of its day as well as for eternity; otherwise we would all have to hate Tiepolo and cling to Fra Angelico.

Author: I'm familiar with the "new movements"—I've had personal and positive experiences with several of them—yet I believe that they would bear more and better fruit if they rediscovered Catholic tradition, as Bishop Marc Aillet and other members of the hierarchy have suggested.[5] We find vitality here and there because God will never let His Church perish. But, like a genetic defect that causes deformities in an otherwise healthy organism, there are human errors mixed in with these movements that have caused and will cause a greater or lesser number of aberrations.

Lady: Can you be more specific? Give me an example?

Author: The Neocatechumenal Way is a movement characterized by profound theological deviations and liturgical distortions.

---

5. See Marc Aillet, "The Sacred Liturgy and the New Communities," in *Sacred Liturgy: The Source and Summit of the Life and Mission of the Church*, ed. Alcuin Reid (San Francisco: Ignatius Press, 2014), 163–82.

Lady: At least we can agree on *that* much. But what of the point I made regarding church music?

Author: There, it seems you have a difficulty not with me but with the Magisterium of the Church, which repeats dozens of times, often quite emphatically, that Gregorian chant, as the music proper to the Roman liturgy, should have the chief place (*principem locum*), and that the pipe organ is the sacred instrument *par excellence*. Naturally, the majority of Catholics ignore such things, just as they ignore the teaching on contraception, on the non-ordainability of women, on the evil of usury, or on the social kingship of Our Lord Jesus Christ.

Lady (*flustered*): That's unfair! You can't equate all these different things. Apples and oranges. And besides, plenty of Catholics...

Author: You mean that you can prove that the majority of Catholics adhere to the Church's teaching on all these matters, or even most of them?

Lady: What do you think proof would look like...

Author: No, you can't. (*Silence.*) Let me just say one last thing, and then I'll need to be going home. As you admitted, and as I can see because you're attending coffee and donuts after High Mass, the Lord bestowed on you a special grace when He led you to discover the riches of the Church's traditional liturgy. There is no need to attack those who are explaining, promoting, and defending that immense liturgical treasury against the barbarians and mad scientists of our era. Love this treasure, learn it better, and lead others to it. You will be doing a favor for them—and for yourself.

Lady: Don't think I'm letting you off the hook. This conversation was hardly finished.

Author: No need to worry. As long as we're both attending the same parish, we're bound to run into each other and keep our weapons bright. "Iron sharpeneth iron." Bye for now. Give my best to your sister.

Lady: I will. Thanks for letting me buttonhole you. Goodbye.

3

"The Old Mass Never Deviates from the Gaze of the Lord"

An Interview with Roseanne T. Sullivan

In your book Noble Beauty, Transcendent Holiness: Why the Modern Age Needs the Mass of Ages *(Angelico Press, 2017), you write as an unabashed apologist for the traditional Latin Mass. You are positive not only that "the Mass of the Ages" is far superior to the new Mass, which Pope Benedict XVI called the Ordinary Form, but also that the Roman Catholic Church as a whole should go back to it. Can you summarize here why the Church should return to the Extraordinary Form?*

The reason is simply that we are debtors to our tradition, we are beholden to our heritage, and we become ungrateful and arrogant wretches when we throw it overboard. The attitude of true humility is to assume that the accumulated wisdom and piety of the Church should continue to guide and inform us. This is how it has always been seen, no matter what century of the Church you look at. It could only have been in the twentieth century, at the pinnacle of evolutionary conceit, that a group of eggheads would have dared lay hands on the rich and subtle worship of the Church to force it into their imaginary categories of relevance or efficiency. Their work was justly punished with desolation and apostasy.

In short, the traditional liturgy expresses the fullness of the Catholic Faith and preserves the piety of Christians intact. This is more than sufficient reason for adhering to it and for insisting that it be the norm, always and everywhere.

And that's why, incidentally, I find "Extraordinary Form" the least satisfactory of all the phrases with which Benedict XVI and others refer to the traditional Latin Mass. One can understand canonically how he arrived at that construct, but it denotes a topsy-turvy conception of the reality and history of liturgy in Western Christendom. The *ordinary* form of our worship has always been some version of the Latin Mass, recognizably in continuity with what we now have in the Missal of 1962 (though not so much with that Missal's Holy Week—that's another story). It is the rite of 1969 that is truly outside of the ordinary course of things.

What are some of the ways the older form of the Roman Rite "expresses the fullness of the Catholic faith," as you say?

The older rite is impressively theocentric, focused on God and the primacy of His Kingdom. It is shot through with words and gestures of self-abasement and penitence, attentive reverence and adoration, acceptance of God's absolute claims upon us. Its prayers and ceremonial bear witness to both the transcendence *and* the immanence of God: He is Emmanuel, God among us, but also the One who dwells in thick darkness, Whom no man has seen or can see. He is our Alpha and Omega, our all in all. The traditional liturgy is uncompromising on this point. Even in what you might call its "instructional" moment, the reading or chanting of Scripture, it remains fixed on the Lord, as if we are not so much reading to ourselves as we are reminding Him of what He said to us—as if we are asking Him to fulfill it again in our midst, according to His promise.

The old Mass never deviates from the gaze of the Lord, always remains under His eye, conscientiously turned to Him. It plunges us into the life-and-death necessity of prayer. Padre Pio said "prayer is the oxygen of the soul." We breathe that oxygen in the old Mass.

Don't we do that in the new Mass, too?

We might do that in the new Mass, but it is much more difficult to do. The oxygen is harder to get. The needs and demands of the spiritual life are muted, swept under the carpet, in this stripped-down vernacular liturgy facing the people, replete with sappy songs, announcements, constant chatter. It was designed to be populocentric, to connect people with one another and with the priest around a table, a meal. As Ratzinger has said, God disappears in such a setup. He may be there on the altar, but the people's minds and hearts are elsewhere. Should we really be surprised that, according to repeated polls, most Catholics who attend the Novus Ordo do not believe in the Real Presence—do not even know that the Church teaches it? The liturgy does not help them to *see*, to *experience*, that truth. It is not just about adequate catechesis. It is about whether the liturgy vividly expresses the truths of the Faith.

To take just one example, the old liturgy's prayers unflinchingly subordinate earthly life to heavenly life; they repudiate the pomps and vanities of fallen secular life. The new liturgy refuses to do this. Its redactors systematically wiped out the old prayers that talked of "despising earthly things" for the sake of heaven.[1] Has there ever been a generation since the creation of Adam and Eve that *more needed* to hear this message than today's? Materialistic hedonism is the broad way along which countless souls are walking to their own destruction—and the Church smiles and waves at them, saying "God bless you."

You say in your book that these problems have to do with a certain attitude towards modernity.

Exactly. Or maybe better, a certain attitude *of* modernity. At its root, modernity is anti-sacral, anti-religious, anti-incarnational, and therefore anti-clerical, anti-ritual, anti-liturgical. You can see this from the many philosophers of the Enlightenment who rejected both divine revelation and organized religion. A few centuries later, we moderns who have imbibed all this philosophical baggage have almost no clue what a solemn, formal, objective, public religious

---

1. See Anthony Cekada, *Work of Human Hands: A Theological Critique of the Mass of Paul VI* (West Chester, OH: Philothea Press, 2010), 219–45. My mention of this exceptionally well-researched study does not signify agreement with the author's conclusions about sacramental validity.

ritual is supposed to look like. We are at a total loss about corporate worship in which the individual ego is subsumed into the greater community of the Church across time and space.

That is why we must hang on to the traditional liturgy for dear life. It is, for all intents and purposes, *pre-modern*—so old that it is unaffected by our contemporary shallowness, biases, prejudices. It breathes a realism, a spaciousness, a strength, a chivalry even, that has become foreign to our age and so, for that very reason, is desperately needed by us. Modern man needs nothing so much as to be delivered from the prison of his Promethean modernism. He needs to be challenged by that which is older, deeper, wiser, stronger, lovelier, happier. He needs to be ignored, not coddled; mystified, not lectured to; silenced, not uncorked.

How did you come to understand these things in your own life?

I grew up in a conventional American parish "in the round." Laity ran everything. The priests preached heterodoxy. The music was atrocious. But I knew no better. I volunteered to do the readings. I joined the choir and sang Marty Haugen songs. I became an Extraordinary Minister of Holy Communion. I was involved in a charismatic youth group and even wrote a guitar song in that style.

Things began to change when I started studying philosophy at the end of high school—most of all, being introduced to Plato and Aristotle. That same year, someone handed me a copy of Ludwig Ott's *Fundamentals of Catholic Dogma*. I remember reading page after page and saying: "So *this* is what the Catholic Church believes? I never knew!" And I caught a glimpse of how beautiful and profound it is.

At Thomas Aquinas College I was introduced to the old Mass and fell in love with it, "love at first sight." It came crashing in on my consciousness as something radically other, glowing with divine transcendence, startling in its complete lack of accommodation to modernity or to me. It did not pander to me but threw down the gauntlet and expected me to submit. The result was a kind of existential sigh of relief: at last, something that is not about me, not catering to me, not desperate for my approval or desperate to bestow approval. It was almost like walking through the wardrobe into Narnia, yet with this difference: the place to which you went was reality, as hard as marble and as soft as silk; it was the unadulterated Gospel, and the place you were leaving was the fantasy, the two-dimensional substitute.

Maybe this was the single greatest discovery I made as I got to know the old Mass (and, eventually, the old Divine Office): its utter objectivity, the grandeur of its own form, the density of its prayer, which paradoxically summoned forth from me the best I could give in return. It was refreshing not to be the center of attention, not to "matter," not to be "active." It led me to a more *interior* activity, a way of relating to the mysteries that I had not so much as suspected during my years of attending the Novus Ordo. Frankly, it was a conversion experience.

Later, as I became more involved in singing chant and polyphony for the Mass (and, in a sense, participating more "actively"), this consciousness of being *fundamentally receptive* at the old Mass never went away. It actually increased as I kept discovering more and more riches in the prayers and rituals of our ancestors. I experienced in a visceral way the truth embedded in the Gradual and Alleluia of the twentieth Sunday after Pentecost. The Gradual says: "The eyes of all hope in Thee, O Lord, and Thou givest them meat in due season. Thou openest Thy hand, and fillest every living creature with Thy blessing."[2] God has prepared a banquet of solid, nourishing, flavorful *meat* in the traditional liturgy—a feast in preparation for over 2,000 years by the time it reaches our altars today. God feeds us and fills us with this liturgy, a sign of which is our receiving holy communion on the tongue and kneeling. Like Mary, we open our souls to receive the mysteries handed down. And then the Alleluia is the exultant response of the banqueter: "Alleluia, alleluia. My heart is ready, O God, my heart is ready. I will sing, and will give praise to Thee, my glory."[3]

And so it is for me today. It is because I seek the fullest possible participation in the mystery of our Lord Jesus Christ, true God and

2. Psalm 144:15–16.
3. Psalm 56:8.

true man, King and High Priest, that I always seek out the old Mass, wherever I may be.

I agree with what you're saying here. But I wonder: What grounds do you have to believe that a return to the Mass of the Ages is even a possibility?

I don't know what the future holds, but right now, looking at the virtual schism in the Catholic Church over basic points of faith and morals, it is hard to escape the conclusion that some mighty upheavals are in the offing, and that many things that might have seemed impossible a short while ago may suddenly become possible.

In my opinion, the movement for Catholic orthodoxy and the movement for liturgical tradition are coming closer together all the time and have already combined in many ways into a single movement. A time will come when Catholics who profess the Niceno-Constantinopolitan Creed, who adhere to the traditional sexual morality of the Church, and who accept priestly celibacy as a discipline willed by the Lord, will be celebrating the *usus antiquior* either exclusively or predominantly. Of course, I have no way of proving this, but let's call it an educated guess.

In any case, we need to have a sound historical perspective based on the study of reform movements in Church history, of which nearly every century has given us shining examples. Every reform movement started with a few people who, rightly scandalized by the faithlessness or immorality of their times and animated with the fervor of divine love, worked tirelessly and organized effectively to promote personal conversion and institutional change. It has always happened this way, and our times will be no exception.

We have to beware of a subtle form of consequentialism, whereby we think we must be doing the right thing because we happen to be successful, or that as long as we do the right thing we cannot fail to be successful. No. We do the right thing even if it's improbable, difficult, quixotic, leads to martyrdom. The success the Lord wants is for souls who care about Him to return to the sacred liturgy in its uncorrupted form, regardless of whether we are supported and applauded for this fidelity, or opposed and persecuted. He will do the rest for us. We are counting not on our superior might or numbers but on *His* resources, His interventions, His multiplication of loaves and fishes. That being said, the traditional movement is in fact growing. All the numbers are there for examination: the numbers of priests and seminarians in traditional orders or communities, as well as the apostolates being entrusted to them, are steadily climbing. The number of families associated with their apostolates is ever on the increase. If someone in the Western world today wants to see a church full of large families, he has to visit traditional communities, for he will hardly find them elsewhere! There is a burgeoning supply of traditionalist books, magazines, pamphlets, catalogs, and religious items, which at least points to a market. Intellectuals and artists, to the extent that the contemporary Church has them, are decidedly favorable to traditionalism.

Let's not kid ourselves: it's the only serious Catholicism there is. The rest is country-club Catholicism at best, and do-it-yourself Catholicism at worst.

When the traditional Latin Mass was made more widely available, many of us hoped that its beauty and reverence would evangelize in and of itself. After ten years, I and others have noted that the Extraordinary Form hasn't achieved much acceptance among people who are attached to the Ordinary Form. Even when it is available, it is often sparsely attended.

For example, more than a year after San Francisco Archbishop Salvatore Cordileone instructed a pastor of the beautiful, centrally located Star of the Sea Church to learn the traditional Latin Mass and start offering it every Sunday before noon, I drove up to the city from where I live in San Jose an hour away, and I saw to my disappointment that very few people actually attend that almost-ideally situated Mass. I am not alone in my observations.

For another example, even when the traditional Latin Mass was offered regularly at Church of Our Savior in New York City by the very well-known Father George W. Rutler, it attracted only a small group, by his own testimony.

As much as it saddens us, this really isn't surprising. In his letter to the world's bishops of July 7, 2007, Pope Benedict XVI said (in a phrase I find pungent, if not caustic): "The use of the old Missal presupposes a certain degree of liturgical formation and some knowledge of the Latin language; neither of these is found very often." Oh, right—you mean the liturgical formation that Vatican II asked clergy and people to prioritize? And the knowledge of Latin that the same Council repeatedly endorsed, and that canon law requires for all clergy prior to ordination?

Put simply: many people are not ready for the royal road. Some, it's true, attend once and are hooked forever, but for others, it's a steep learning curve. They are the victims of such bad liturgical practices and habits that they will not know what to do with themselves when suddenly up against the edge of an infinite chasm of prayer, with no one to hold their hand, and a ritual that unfolds with what may look like a lofty indifference or a chilly remoteness. It can be severely disturbing to your average Catholic.

This is why, by the way, I always say that if you want to bring someone to a Tridentine Mass, you should bring him to a *Missa cantata* or even a Solemn High Mass, if you can find one nearby. The High Mass is far easier to relate to, as it appeals to all the senses, and carries the worshiper along on a gentle stream.

Yes, I can see your point. So, you think it's unfair to say that the traditional Latin Mass is a "boutique phenomenon" among American Catholics?

Let's wait till it's readily available in every diocese, over a span of many years, and then we can reassess the question of whether it has wide appeal...

But coming back to what I said a moment ago: the Latin Mass is hard-core, full-on Catholicism, no holds barred. The liturgy is longer and more elaborate. The music is likely be the real stuff: Gregorian chant, polyphony. The preaching is also likely to be tougher, closer to what you'd expect from a religion that claims to be divinely revealed as the only way to salvation. Women are wearing mantillas, people are dressed formally. The whole package is radically opposed to the *mores* of contemporary Americans, including, sadly, Catholics themselves, who are contracepting and divorcing at pretty nearly the same rate as their heathen counterparts. I hate to say it, but the dominant ersatz version of Catholicism really *is* like a different religion, compared to the historic, authentic, dogmatic, ascetical-mystical Catholicism embodied in the traditional liturgy and the devotions that flourish in its ambit. So, do we call this a "boutique phenomenon," or do we have the courage to admit that Catholicism is in a state of accelerating decomposition and that most of what the world calls "Catholicism" is a shadow of the reality, if not a contradiction of it?

But let's be honest about this, too: the main reason the old Mass has not caught on more is the lack of availability and the lack of ecclesiastical support. Pope Benedict liberated it for the benefit of all priests and for the faithful they serve, but a huge number of priests have been cajoled, threatened, ostracized, or removed from ministry due to conflicts over *Summorum Pontificum.* I know what I am talking about from firsthand experience. Too many bishops and pastors are opposed to it, and the young clergy who can already do the old liturgy or who may wish to learn it are kept down, forced into the mold of the postconciliar revolution. The lack of growth to which you refer is the result of a deliberate strategy of "containment" that is discussed and implemented at the level of episcopal conferences. Not officially, mind you, but behind closed doors.

Thanks be to God there are still some heroic bishops and priests here and there who, in spite of all the political pressure, manage to hold their own line and promote the recovery of liturgical tradition in their dioceses or parishes. It is happening, slowly, across the face of the earth—I have been to many such places and seen the lively faith of clergy and laity. But it could and should be happening *everywhere.* There is an artificial limitation being imposed by monopolists. If we had a "free market economy," so to speak, we would be looking at a far different picture.

Again, this situation is not unprecedented, either in salvation history or in Church history (which itself follows, again and again, the pattern of salvation history). Remember the story of Gideon in chapter 7 of the Book of Judges? He had with him 32,000 troops to go up against the Midianites. The Lord said to him: "The people with you are too many for me to give the Midianites into their hand, lest Israel vaunt themselves against me, saying, 'My own hand has delivered me.'" So the Lord made sure he lowered the number first to 10,000, then to 300. With these "picked men," Gideon obtained total victory over his enemies, who were "like locusts for multitude." The God of Abraham, Isaac, and Jacob seems to have a preference for winning improbable victories, so that the glory can be His and not ours. "Not to us, O Lord, not to us, but to Thy Name give glory." I take much comfort in this.

The odds of the traditional Latin Mass replacing the Mass of 1969 seem to me to be vanishingly remote, so I've been afraid that what traditionalists are advocating is like so much shouting into the wind.

But then I chanced upon this, written by a secular blogger: "Anything worth shouting about is worth shouting into the wind. Because if enough people care, often enough, the word spreads, the standards change, the wind dies down. If enough people care, the culture changes. It's easy to persuade ourselves that the right time to make change happen is when it's time. But that's never true. The right time to make it happen is before it's time. Because this is what 'making' means. . . . Yes, there's wind, there's always been wind. But that doesn't mean we should stop shouting."

I couldn't agree more, except that I'd say we don't always have to be shouting. We need to practice the art of persuasion, good advertising, and, obviously, best behavior. The take-away is that we have a *lot* of work to do in winning our brothers and sisters over to traditional Catholicism, for their own good and for the health of the Church.

This is going to happen to some extent naturally as things get worse and worse in the Church and in the world. People who are serious about the Faith will ask: "Where is this Faith being taught and lived? Where is there a priest who believes and preaches the Faith? Where is the liturgy being celebrated in a way that nourishes and strengthens my faith?" We need to be there for them when they start asking these questions, and not drive them away because they are initially poorly dressed, or kneel at the wrong times, or sing badly, or have confused ideas. I have this image in my mind of traditional Catholicism as a field hospital in which many wandering pagans and lukewarm believers will find healing, convalescence, and robust health.

You write that lots of young seminarians and newly ordained priests have learned to celebrate the traditional Latin Mass, and you are hopeful about that. I am too. But recently some liberals are saying that the tradition-loving, cassock-wearing seminarians who came in during Benedict's reign might be supplanted by a newer wave of priests influenced by Pope Francis.

I imagine this is true to some extent. But again, I think it would not be so much a swinging of the pendulum as the ongoing residue of postconciliar confusion, which has polluted nearly everyone's thinking. Moreover, if progressives are in charge of seminaries, they know very well how to filter out the "excessively rigid" candidates—you know, those who believe the *Catechism*, pray the rosary, kneel for communion, and such things. Hence, in some seminaries the "Francis Effect" will certainly show itself as the rejection or dismissal of perfectly acceptable but "rigid" candidates.

Remember, for a dyed-in-the-wool liberal, the worst Church is one populated by traditional Catholics. They would rather board up the doors of every single church and have no more sacraments than return to the *usus antiquior*. They are *at war* with tradition.

Nevertheless, the shift in mentality ushered in by Benedict XVI should not be underestimated. He elevated the Church's intellectual, spiritual, and liturgical profile to a level it had not enjoyed since before the Council, and left behind a treasure-trove of writings, particularly on the sacred liturgy, that will be read for decades and possibly centuries to come. The "Benedict Effect" may be quieter, but it's deeper and more pervasive. Wherever you find a diocese bursting with vocations and Mass attendance, you will find the Ratzingerian influence at work.

I know a priest who gradually removed most of the liturgical abuses in

*his parish over almost a decade, with much more patience than I could
have shown, and for all his pains, he received a lot of rancor. Eventually, in spite of all his patient catechesis of his parishioners, the priest
was removed by his religious superior. All this happened under a sup-
portive bishop. I fear to think what new tradition-minded priests will
face in their parishes after ordination.*

Yes, I don't want to seem like a Pollyanna who is downplaying the
difficulties. They are very real. For one thing, the persecution of
orthodox Catholics is getting worse under this pontificate. Anyone
who questions *Amoris Laetitia,* for example, is instantly *persona non
grata.* A priest who preaches against homosexuality or contraception from the pulpit might well be "disciplined." And a priest who
starts offering the Latin Mass might as well tape a bullseye on the
back of his shirt, with the words "Shoot me!" But this cannot and
will not be the final word. We are only in one phase of a long battle.
No pope and no bishop lasts forever; generations come and go,
some problems disappear and others arise to take their place.

This much is clear: the priests who are faithful to their sacerdotal
ministry, who preach the truth "in season and out of season," who
offer the liturgy with utmost reverence, who make the tradition
come alive again: these priests will be blessed even in the midst of
many crosses, and will become a blessing to their people. Our Lord
will take care of them and make of them what He will. I know
priests who have gone through terrible situations, which were the
prelude to their arrival in a better place, to do more important
work. We have to have confidence that God will take care of His
own when they do what they are supposed to do.

I know a priest who has been punished for his stance on never
giving communion to people in the hand, because it goes against
his conscience to see the Body of Our Lord handled in that casual
way, with the danger of particles being lost (not to mention the loss
of faith in the Real Presence and the loss of faith in the ontological
distinction between the ordained and the non-ordained). I admire
him and others like him. They are the grain of wheat that will fall
into the ground and die, so that an abundant harvest can spring
forth.

I would also say that young men discerning a priestly vocation need to be wise as serpents and innocent as doves (cf. Mt 10:16). They should think about whether it would not be better for them to join a society of apostolic life or a religious community that utilizes only the old liturgical books. These books are repositories of the Church's tradition. And the priests who are bound to their use will not normally face the same kind of opposition and maltreatment that the secular clergy too often do. I would say something similar, incidentally, to young women discerning a religious vocation—indeed, it is even more important for them to join a community that will be served exclusively by priests who offer the *usus antiquior.* Let us beg the Lord on our knees to send laborers into the harvest!

Do you think there is a danger of discouragement in the ranks of traditional Catholics?

Absolutely. You run into it everywhere. Faithful people are especially scandalized by what's happening in the upper ranks of the Church, and they are predicting that the sky will fall in on our heads. Maybe it will, but that's still not the end of the world. Nor will it be the end of us, either.

We have to fight hard against discouragement. Saint Thérèse said: "Discouragement is a form of pride."[4] It is pride in the sense that we start second-guessing Divine Providence and blaming the Lord for not intervening or solving this or that problem as we would have done. But God *is* in charge, and His ways are *not* our ways. Our job is to do, as well as we can, whatever He has given us the light and strength to do. We all know the famous words of Mother Teresa: "We are called upon not to be successful, but to be faithful." God will bless and multiply the good of our fidelity to Him, to the Church, to Catholic tradition, whether we see the fruits of it in our lifetime or not.

This past August [2017], Pope Francis stated that there is no possibility

---

4. "Prayer for Acquiring Humility," in *The Prayers of Saint Thérèse of Lisieux,* trans. Aletheia Kane, OCD (Washington, DC: ICS Publications, 1997), 116.

of rethinking the decisions behind the liturgical changes; all we should do now is seek to understand the reasons why they were made. He said: "We can affirm with certainty and magisterial authority that the liturgical reform is irreversible."[5] What do you make of this?

It is not easy to understand what the Holy Father expects to accomplish with this sentence, as it is not a doctrinal statement but an evaluation of a contingent historical fact, namely, the process of reform that began after *Sacrosanctum Concilium* and culminated in the various Novus Ordo liturgical books. It's like saying: "The euro is irreversibly established in Europe." Why should we think so? Or: "The ecumenism of the past fifty years is an irreversible fact." Sure, no one can deny that it has *happened*, and as such, cannot be undone. But that doesn't say anything about what the future holds; nor does it say that, with the wisdom of hindsight, we may not judge this irreversible *fact* of five decades of ecumenism to have been an error of which we should repent as quickly and as thoroughly as possible. The whole thing, new liturgical rites or ecumenism or whatever, could be scrapped, or at least severely "corrected," by a forthcoming Leo XIV or Benedict XVII or Pius XIII.

In reality, the only thing irreversible about the liturgical reform is its datedness, its failure to connect with the deeper needs of modern man—something that was predicted even in the 1960's by many who could read well the signs of the times. Meanwhile, traditional parishes and communities are thriving with young people. *That* is the really interesting sign of the times.

One might also note that one pope (Clement VII) authorized the creation of a novel breviary designed by Cardinal Quiñones, another pope (Paul III) issued it, and yet a third (Paul IV) suppressed it, deeming it a rupture in the tradition and excessively influenced by Protestant theology. Popes actually can get the liturgy wrong. Councils, too, are by no means infallible when it comes to recommendations about practical things to be done or not done. No one questions that the Council Fathers desired minor changes to the liturgy, but many notable authors, including Joseph Ratzinger

---

5. Address to Participants in the 68th National Liturgical Week, August 24, 2017.

and Louis Bouyer, have raised serious questions about the manner in which these changes were carried out.

To put it in a nutshell, this speech on liturgical reform was as incoherent as many other speeches of this pontificate, such as the one in October 2017 on how the death penalty is *"per se* contrary to the Gospel." One has to shrug one's shoulders, throw up one's hands, pull out one's beads, and say: "O Lord, how long?"

Thank you for this interview. I am especially happy that you were willing to frankly address some of the problems that troubled me when I was reading your eloquent and persuasive essays in Noble Beauty, Transcendent Holiness. *As you said, "many things that might have seemed impossible a short while ago may suddenly become possible." And I agree, we do have to fight hard against discouragement. We have to be humble and holy ourselves so that God can work through us to obtain His purposes. I hope and pray that many readers will also find in your book, as I have done, much to think about, much to be consoled about, and much to be strengthened by.*

4

On Liturgical Development and Corruption

The following dialogue occurs between a traditionalist and a Catholic of good will who has started attending the old Mass but is still trying to understand the traditionalist's position.

Oliver: Charlie, I've often heard you say that the Novus Ordo represents a huge rupture with the preceding liturgical tradition. But you never comment about *other* changes in the history of liturgy, like the development of the whispered low Mass, that also break with preceding tradition—I guess because traditionalists are okay with these things. So what's the difference? When is a new direction not truly a rupture? Or is it a "development" if you happen to agree with it, and a "rupture" if you happen to dislike it?

Charles: Great question. I would say that developments come in two basic "flavors": those that flow forth in harmony with something profoundly within the liturgy, like a flower from a tree, and those that are imposed from without in a mechanistic way, like a prosthetic limb.

Oliver: Could you illustrate your distinction in reference to the low Mass example?

Charles: The liturgy is certainly meant to be sung in its solemn form—you, of all people, know I've defended that many times.[1]

1. See P. Kwasniewski, *Noble Beauty, Transcendent Holiness*, ch. 10: "The Peace of Low Mass and the Glory of High Mass."

However, the mystery of the Mass also allows for and invites the priest into an intense mysticism of intercession, oblation, and communion. Thus, it is easy to see how, especially in monastic settings with an abundance of priests, the private daily Mass emerged in contradistinction to the conventual or parochial Mass. This need not be seen as a problem, unless it becomes the norm for communal Mass and edges out the sung liturgy.

Oliver: But how would you defend the proposition that this change was incidental and not substantive?

Charles: One might say that the same Mass exists at different levels of execution, like the difference between a Shakespeare play read quietly to oneself, the same play read aloud by a group of friends, and the play fully acted out in costume on the stage with props and so forth. It is the same play, but realized more or less fully according to its essence as a play. Any one of those actualizations of the play is based on one and the same play. Think how different it would be if instead you had a modernized redaction of Shakespeare that purged Catholic references so as not to offend Protestants, changed the vocabulary to contemporary English, and changed the gender of the starring roles! In this case, even if the play was given the same title, it would no longer be the same reality—no matter how well you acted it out on stage.

Oliver: I see what you're getting at. But here's something that's bothered me. How long does it take until something can be considered part of ecclesiastical tradition? If a parish has communion in the hand for forty years, does this then become part of tradition? Imagine if—God forbid!—altar girls are the norm for the next hundred years. In the year 2118, can one look back and say, "this is not and never has been ecclesiastical tradition," or would one say, "this *is* a tradition, but it's bad and we should change it"?

Charles: Let's take up the question of communion first. When the Latin Church shifted in the Middle Ages to communion under the species of bread alone, given on the tongue to faithful who are kneeling, it was for good reasons: it fosters a spirit of humility and adoration, and, on a practical level, is easier and safer. It is, in other words, completely in accord with the letter and spirit of the liturgical action, something that emerges from a deeper grasp of the mystery of the Holy Eucharist. Therefore, there could never be a compelling reason to undo this development, unless we wanted *less* safety, *less* humility, and *less* adoration. But that could only come from the devil. In fact, Paul VI himself recognized that communion on the tongue was superior and reasserted it,[2] although he then allowed the abuse of communion in the hand to sweep over the Church because he was an indecisive and confused shepherd—even his best decisions still have something of Hamlet mixed in with them, as when he called a commission to look into birth control and the pill, which raised false hopes among the progressives. But I digress...

Oliver: So you don't buy the argument that it was good to restore communion in the hand because "it's what used to be done in ancient times"?

Charles: This both begs the question—why did the custom change if it was so good to begin with?—*and* contradicts the teaching of Pope Pius XII that we should avoid antiquarianism, i.e., returning to an older practice just because it's older.[3] When an early custom was universally left behind and another put in its place, we should see this as a recognition of the latter's superiority.

Oliver: Would this apply to the Novus Ordo as well, since it was universally put in place of the old rite of Mass?

Charles: Of course not. First, thanks to the protection of the Holy Spirit, Paul VI, who wanted to abolish the old liturgy, never success-

---

2. In the Instruction *Memoriale Domini* on the Manner of Distributing Holy Communion (May 29, 1969).
3. See *Mediator Dei*, nn. 59–64.

fully abrogated it, as Pope Benedict XVI later acknowledged.[4] So the old liturgy has always remained legitimate (and, indeed, it could never be otherwise). Moreover, while the Tridentine liturgical books were eventually received universally, the Novus Ordo was resisted from the beginning by an intrepid number of clergy and laity, and this refusal to accept the rupture has not faded away but has actually grown over the decades. In this way it is simply a fact that the Novus Ordo, while unfortunately the predominant rite, cannot be said to have supplanted and replaced the old rite, whereas communion on the tongue to kneeling faithful *totally* replaced any other manner of reception in the Middle Ages. Thus one cannot, in principle or in practice, make the argument that the more recent rite is superior to the more ancient rite. But one would have to say quite a bit more on this matter, and maybe we are drifting from the main point...

Oliver: Let me ask a general question. Why don't you think there should be continual change in the liturgy—you know, different things for different ages and peoples?

Charles: I recognize that there can and will be small changes, like the addition of new feasts or saints to the calendar, or new prefaces, but not large-scale changes. Church history shows that development starts out at a more rapid pace and slows down increasingly as the liturgy reaches perfection. In a way, it is like molten lava that erupts from a fissure and gradually cools to become solid. In the same way, the liturgy gushed forth from the heart of Jesus on the Cross, and solidified over the centuries as holy men and women continued to pray it, showing great reverence to what they inherited from their predecessors.

Oliver: The Byzantine Divine Liturgy, for instance, has changed very little over the last several centuries, and the great majority of East-

---

4. In the letter to bishops accompanying the motu proprio *Summorum Pontificum*: "As for the use of the 1962 Missal as a *Forma extraordinaria* of the liturgy of the Mass, I would like to draw attention to the fact that this Missal was never juridically abrogated and, consequently, in principle, was always permitted."

ern Christians see no need to change it, since it accomplishes so well what it exists for.

Charles: Exactly. The traditional Roman liturgy grew to its mature grandeur more slowly than did the Byzantine, but the same progressive solidification and the same conservative instinct can be seen in it. The Roman Canon was complete by the start of the seventh century; then most of the remaining ceremonies by the early Middle Ages; and finally the prayers at the foot of the altar and the Last Gospel in the late Middle Ages. At this point it no longer needed to evolve and could remain solid and stable for almost 500 years (from 1570 to 1962). Those who use it today see no need to "develop" it further; on the contrary, they unanimously wish to keep the Mass in its fullness, prior to the corruptions introduced by Pius XII after 1948.

Oliver: Wait a minute—I thought you liked Pius XII. What's this I'm hearing?

Charles: With any modern pope one has to make distinctions. Pius XII as a theoretician is generally sound and often incisive. Pius XII as a reformer couldn't quite escape the *Zeitgeist*. He put into place the mechanisms that would lead to the evisceration of the Roman rite.

Oliver: I've never heard that before; in my circles this pope is simply the hero of the World War II period and a great anti-Modernist like Pius X. I mean, look at *Humani Generis*! But I am definitely interested in hearing more, as I've discovered over the years that the popular narrative is usually wrong. But let's keep our focus for now on the liturgical question and come back to Pacelli another time.

Charles: Fine with me.

Oliver: I know that some people compare the process of maturation you were describing a moment ago to the way a human being develops. Do you think that analogy holds? It seems like one would run into the problem of aging and senility…

Charles: Rightly understood, this analogy works. A child changes tremendously on the way to adulthood, but the pace of change becomes less as time goes on. Everyone knows that one year of time means something very different in the first 10 years of life, the second 10 years, and the remaining decades. Time, for organic things, is not simple and undifferentiated. And if we were not fallen beings, we might remain adults at approximately age 33 for our entire lives. The liturgy grows to maturity and then remains at maturity, without fail, until the second coming of Christ. Hence, a strange custom that arises in the twentieth or twenty-first century cannot lay claim to being a natural development but is more like a cancerous tumor in a body. It is like an infantilization, a rejection of maturity.

Oliver: But what do you make of my altar girl example? What if we had them for over a century?

Charles: As St Athanasius says, even if the whole world agreed that Christ was not God, the handful of Christians who still worshiped Him as God would be correct; they would *be* the Church. "They have the buildings, you have the Faith," he famously said to the small band of anti-Arian Catholics. Similarly, even if we were to have altar girls for 200 years, they would *always* be an aberration of the Western liturgical tradition, and *never* an organic development. A machine is a machine; it will never turn into an organism. Schizophrenia will always be a disorder, no matter how long one has it. A man is a man and a woman a woman, regardless of what the confused gender-ideology of the day wants to say about it.

Oliver: That makes a lot of sense.

Charles: And by the way, you have to resist a lie that has gained a great deal of ground, namely that matters of liturgy are on a different plane than matters of doctrine. Someone might say, "disputes about the divinity of Christ are one thing; disagreements about the liturgical discipline of altar servers are quite another. Don't lump together Arius and Bugnini, or Honorius and Paul VI." But in reality, *every* liturgical question stems from and resolves to a doctrinal question. Nothing we do in our worship is doctrinally neutral or irrelevant or inconsequential.

Oliver: That certainly seems true, if you just look at the shift in the beliefs of ordinary Catholics from preconciliar to postconciliar times. The next logical question, I guess, would be this: How do we know what stage of development the Church is in right now? I could imagine the faithful in the fifteenth century saying: "A strange custom that arises in the fifteenth century cannot lay claim to being a natural development but is more like a tumor." And are not some innovations, such as the centralized tabernacle on the altar, considered to be non-tumorous changes even though they did not come about until rather late?

Charles: Perhaps the solution to this conundrum is to look at *why* people make the changes they make. In the fifteenth century—or, for that matter, any century—liturgy tends to be developed in the direction of *expansion*. People *add* processions, litanies, extra prayers, repetitions. They do this out of devotion. It is rare that such things are pruned, though it does happen from time to time. However, what is absolutely unprecedented is for *very many things* to be cut back simultaneously and as a result of utilitarian, rationalist, and activist presuppositions, as occurred in the 1960's. So I think one can see a crucial difference between earlier phases of development, which involve positive growth, and the contrary motion of corruption, which is opposed to that growth and in fact tends to hate it and attack it iconoclastically—always a sign of the Evil One. When altars got bigger and grander, it was a development. When altars were jackhammered and dumped, it was a rupture.

Oliver: How is one to know that some change ought to be made?

Charles: Anything that belongs to the practical order will involve the exercise of the virtue of prudence: we are making a judgment about what it is prudent to change. But always with a tremendous, even fearful respect for all that has been received in tradition! That is why the Second Vatican Council, in one of its more sober statements, said: "There must be no innovations unless the good of the Church genuinely and certainly requires them; and care must be taken that any new forms adopted should in some way grow organically from forms already existing."[5] The Council Fathers were mostly pastors of souls, and they knew that too much change at any time, for any reason, is a bad thing, as St Thomas explains when discussing why even laws that are imperfect should not necessarily be replaced with better laws, because it weakens the confidence people have in habitually following laws in general.[6]

Oliver: Of course, bringing back the old Latin liturgy is a change of custom for most Catholics, so it, too, could weaken their sense of ecclesial stability or trust. What do you say to that?

Charles: The only justification that can be given for such a big change is that the good of recovering liturgical tradition overwhelmingly outweighs the evil of disturbing people's habits.[7] Besides, churchmen since the Second Vatican Council have given us so many reasons to distrust their decisions that it's rather silly at this point to suggest that we can be destabilized more than we have already been by all the doctrinal confusion, moral laxity, and liturgical chaos of the past five decades. The return of tradition means a return of dogma, holiness, and right worship—all *stabilizing* factors. It's like going from anarchy to government, or from a starvation diet to a royal banquet. Only a cruel person would say: "The poor are so accustomed to malnutrition that we should just let them stay at that level, even though we are capable of providing them with abundant nutrition."

Oliver: Your arguments make me wonder about the use and abuse of Church authority. Would you say there was a similar (although not nearly as bad) problem when the Council of Trent suppressed rites? It seems to me that after Trent the idea of what the liturgy is in relation to the Vatican undergoes a shift.

---

5. *Sacrosanctum Concilium*, n. 23.
6. St Thomas Aquinas, *Summa theologiae* I-II, q. 97, art. 2.
7. Ibid.

On Liturgical Development and Corruption

Charles: Yes, Trent, or perhaps I should say St Pius V, did introduce a new dynamic. He did not abolish any rite older than 200 years, but the way the new missal was imposed showed a tendency to overreach.

Oliver: One can sympathize with St Pius V; it was a centralized response to the centrifugal force of Protestant experimentation and fragmentation.

Charles: For sure. I don't deny that. But in 1570, for the first time in history, a pope took upon himself the role of officially promulgating a missal for the Latin-rite Church. It's quite striking, isn't it, to think that Catholicism endured for 1,500 years with a rich liturgical tradition that had *never* been administered or validated by the Vatican?

Oliver: The only thing more striking, one could say, is that Paul VI was audacious enough to introduce a *new* missal, which Pius V would never have done, or even conceived of doing. His 1570 missal was, for all intents and purposes, the same as papal curial missals had been for centuries before.

Charles: You are provoking me, aren't you, to take up the question of whether or not Paul VI's manufactured liturgy can seriously be called the Roman rite, and whether or not this talk of "two forms" can really be defended… That's a longer conversation, for another day. But this much should give us pause: never in the history of the Catholic Church had there been a *new missal*, until 1969.

Oliver: Whatever the answer may be, it won't change where I'll be heading for church on Sunday. See you at the High Mass for the Sixth Sunday after Pentecost!

Charles: You bet.

5

"Where Angels Chant Before the Pierced and Glorified Lamb"

An Interview with the Latin Mass Society of England & Wales

Why did you write your book Resurgent in the Midst of Crisis?

We are living through a crisis of an unprecedented nature—one that affects the Church no less than the world at large. The crisis is characterized by a systematic, all-encompassing rebellion against tradition and the wisdom of the ages, against divine revelation, even against human reason and natural law, as Pope Benedict XVI often said.

I believe what many mystics and theologians have believed: the battle between Christ and Antichrist, between the Spirit of Truth and the hedonistic, nihilistic spirit of modernity, is intensifying and will continue to escalate until the Second Coming. The sides are drawn up with increasing clarity and there is a certain massive inevitability about the forces of total secularization. We are in a new era of persecution, but with the strange twist that the persecution also happens *within* the Church against her faithful, like an autoimmune disease. Curiously, it was none other than Pope Paul VI who bore witness to the "smoke of Satan" that had "entered the temple of God."[1] Because of the immutable law of the Cross—the blood of martyrs is the seed of Christianity—Satan can never crush the

---

1. Homily for the Solemnity of the Holy Apostles Peter and Paul and the Ninth Anniversary of the Coronation of His Holiness, June 29, 1972. The Italian original, a third-person summary, may be found at the Vatican website.

Church, although surely he can be permitted to test her and bring about a purification on a scale never seen before.

The battle in the Roman Church between those who love the age-old traditional liturgy and those who have rejected it and replaced it with a banal fabrication is but one of several "fronts" in that intensifying conflict, and yet it is a particularly central one, because both symbolically and ontologically the liturgy is the center of our Faith. How it is offered up to God, how we enter into it in faith, how we are formed by it in charity, determines the rest of the complexion and course of Christianity.

When the liturgy is received humbly and its inner dynamism is lived to the full, the Church militant flourishes in sanctity and the rest of her house comes to be in order, no matter how great the surrounding chaos; but to the extent that people blithely or blindly follow along the course of rupture and discontinuity, the house will suffer confusion, will waste away to utter irrelevancy. The Church in many parts of the world has made a pathetic parody of herself, whoring after ephemeral worldly relevance, tithing the mint and cumin while neglecting the weightier matters of righteousness. The surrender to utilitarianism has resulted in the just punishment of a simultaneous loss of our powerful means of sanctification and a failure to achieve the end of reaching modern man, who is more desperate than ever for an escape from the prison of modernity.

That is why, for me, nothing is more important than defending and promoting the venerable Roman Rite (and, for that matter, all kindred traditional rites, Eastern and Western), and critiquing openly and plainly the harmful deviations that have afflicted the Church's life of worship, especially in the past half-century. We have done things to our inheritance, to the most fundamental expressions of the Catholic religion, that would have been literally unimaginable to our predecessors in any age; we have set up an abomination of desolation in the temple, and we are suffering grievously for it.

God in His inscrutable Providence has permitted bad shepherds to be placed over the flock, to mislead, abuse, and persecute it. In the midst of these woes, it is a true cause for rejoicing to see an ever-growing movement of Catholic laity and clergy who are rising up against the mediocrity, the flagrant denial of reality, the worldliness

and empty slogans, the poisonous modernism, and who are rightfully and reasonably demanding the restoration of the inheritance
of the Faith in all its sacrality, holiness, and beauty. Belonging to
Our Lord Jesus Christ, this inheritance can never die, though we
may temporarily lose sight of it; belonging to us as our birthright in
baptism, it was handed down to us by holy ancestors so that we
might faithfully transmit it to all generations to come, until the Lord
returns. We are not going to relinquish it or roll over and play dead.

My book is a lively expression of all these convictions. How are
we to worship God in spirit and in truth, in our day, in our tradition, with all the riches at our disposal, and in spite of all the chaos?
Why is the traditional Roman Rite the way forward, the unswerving
way out of the disaster? What are the crippling problems that beset
the new liturgy, making it poorly suited for the New Evangelization?
These are the sorts of questions that drove the writing of the chapters of this book. I find it a tremendously difficult and exciting time
to be alive and to be part of the traditionalist movement, which is a
movement of youth, serious piety, gritty determination, joyful discovery, and hope against hope.

*In your view, what is it about the traditional liturgy that keeps attract-
ing adherents, old and new?*

The classical liturgy is so obviously focused on God. The whole
thing, from beginning to end, is an act of adoration, praise, thanksgiving, and supplication directed to Him. There is no doubt what-
soever that the priest is "busy about the Father's business,"[2] as was
the young Jesus in the temple, and that the faithful, too, accompany
him along the way of Calvary as he offers the supreme sacrifice. It is
all focused on the spiritual, the divine, the transcendent, the mystery. You can see it, hear it, feel it.

Indeed, if you're not accustomed to the old Mass, you can feel
positively naked, awkward, out of place, as if you've trespassed into
someone's private rooms. There is a tremendous air of secrecy and a
humbling disregard for the people who happen to be there. I don't

---

2. Luke 2:49.

mean in any uncharitable sense, but just that it's not about you, it's not about me, it's totally about *Him.* By His mercy, we get to be there and participate in *His* mystery, His awesome work of redemption—we are drawn into that height, rather than drawing God down to our level.

As I said, the entire feel of the traditional liturgy is quite different from the man-centered, horizontally tilted community worship of the reformed rite, where it's disturbingly easy to forget that one is assisting at the Holy Sacrifice of the Mass. At a Tridentine High Mass or Solemn Mass, one can be carried away to the timeless worship of the heavenly Jerusalem, where angels chant one to the other before the pierced and glorified Lamb. At a Low Mass, the tranquility, the extremely rich prayers, and the poignant gestures can plunge a person into deep meditation on the mysteries of the Lord and His entourage, the saints.

There is so much one could say, but in essence, I believe that what attracts adherents is the naked confrontation with the Holy. If you are longing for that, you will respond to it. If you are scared of it, you will not darken the door.

So you maintain that there is a resurgence of interest in the Old Rite. What would you say is the evidence for it? And how is this not a form of disobedience to the Church of today?

Obviously there are ups and downs, progress here and setbacks there; the resurgence is a checkered history of victories and disappointments. The traditionalist movement—which, it is important to say, supports and promotes far more than the old Mass: it embraces the Divine Office, devotions like the Rosary, priestly and religious life lived with maximum density and consistency, and what might be called "child-friendly family life," including homeschooling—is of course strong and flourishing in America right now, and stronger in Anglophone countries in general than in others. Continental Europe has pockets of traditional Catholic life, as manifested in conferences and workshops, growing religious communities, excellent publications, and new apostolates. South America, Africa, and Asia have their pockets as well.

The most obvious indicator, I suppose, is simply that as each year passes, more and more parishes and chapels offer the traditional Latin Mass. It is becoming easier to find a good Mass to attend while traveling, and one meets more young clergy who either already know how to celebrate the TLM or wish to learn it. As time goes on, the Priestly Fraternity of Saint Peter and similar societies are entrusted with more apostolates. Any sane bishop who cares about the practice of the Faith is going to think: "If this will get Catholics faithfully attending Mass and living out their Christian duties, by all means, let it happen!" I don't know if this trend will continue, given the chillier atmosphere at the moment, but I think it will be hard to stop the momentum that's been building, especially since *Summorum Pontificum*.

The cause of this resurgence is twofold. The number-one reason is quite simply the ongoing desire of the most serious of practicing Catholics to get as far away as possible from the distracting humanism and horizontalism, the irreverence, informality, saccharine music, and general atmosphere of noise that plague the reformed liturgy. This also explains the unusual phenomenon of Roman Catholics in America who have more or less "gone Byzantine" by attaching themselves to the nearest Ukrainian, Ruthenian, Melkite, Maronite (etc.) parish.

A second reason, I believe, is the ever-increasing literacy about the botched reform, its dubious or modernist principles, and the contrasting beauty of the traditional forms of worship, due to books, articles, conferences, and especially online resources, including the photos and videos one might see at a site like *New Liturgical Movement*. Things that had been hidden away from the faithful for half a century are suddenly on display and advertised as scheduled in this or that city or parish. Bugnini said that the liturgical reform, to be successful, would need two generations of Catholics who knew only the new Mass. Thanks be to God, this never happened, as the old Mass never ceased to be celebrated any day of any year since the Second Vatican Council.

Of course, none of this would be possible without the heroic witness and pioneering labors of men like Eric de Saventhem, Dietrich von Hildebrand, and Michael Davies, who kept alive the flame of hope in the darkest hour, and who, against unbelievable odds, strove with popes, cardinals, and bishops for the retention of the traditional liturgy. Their stance has been vindicated and their legacy has borne abundant fruit.

If I might be permitted a digression: some Catholics who debate with me maintain that the Novus Ordo Missae, because it was promulgated by Paul VI for the entire Church, is *de facto* the Church's current liturgy, and that the *usus antiquior* is a kind of exception or concession permitted for the good of a limited portion of the faithful. If, however, one sign of a successfully promulgated liturgy is its universal and voluntary acceptance by the faithful, we may certainly say that the Novus Ordo Missae was not altogether successfully promulgated, for two reasons: its use has precisely coincided with the greatest decline in the history of the Church in the number of Mass attendees, and, further, the use of the traditional Roman Rite that it was intended to replace has never ceased and is now steadily increasing.

We could add several other observations: the Anglican Ordinariate liturgy, which has restored many elements of the calendar, text, and ceremonial of the pre-Bugnini liturgy; the continuing conferral of minor orders, which Paul VI attempted to suppress; the praying of Prime in monastic communities, even though it was "abolished"; and so forth. In other words, the *usus antiquior* was not reformed, but rather, a new liturgy was put in its place, and while the vast majority follow the new liturgy, it enjoys by no means universal and unquestioned adherence.

Indeed, one might ask the question whether there is even such a thing as "*the* new liturgy," since the celebration of it varies so much from country to country, diocese to diocese, church to church, even priest to priest, and its inherent variability makes it not so much a *rite* as a *schema* of worship to be filled in at the discretion of the clergy and community.

Is such resurgence as you describe flying in the face of the general movement of the Church?

I don't know; it's hard to tell what the general movement is nowadays, things are so very chaotic and nebulous. Is there a *general* movement? Pope Francis has had paradoxical effects: his words and actions have prompted some conservatives to adopt or sympathize with a more traditional perspective, while making others *less* friendly to traditionalists who fearlessly call a spade a spade and warn against the trend towards soft modernism. Some liberals adore him, others are sharpening their knives because he is not delivering on his initial promise of turning the Faith upside-down.

I get the impression, as do so many others, of an increasing polarization—which certainly has something to do with the eschatological battle to which I was referring earlier. One thinks of the contrast between Cardinal George and Archbishop [now Cardinal] Cupich. Those who are traditional and those who are "progressive" will reach a point where they do not share the same faith or practice the same religion. In a way, the Synod[3] has been a good thing for showing people's true colors, for setting in stark contrast the Catholicism that holds fast to what has always been taught and the pseudo-Catholicism that sells a birthright for a mess of pottage.

For me, it's oddly hopeful to think about the fact that liberal Catholicism is suicidal. The Gospel of Modernity churches are emptying out, and a self-serving bureaucracy is an unsustainable enterprise. For these reasons, even if there seems to be a "general movement" in the Church *away* from tradition, it's a race of lemmings to see who gets to the cliff first.

What do the Synod in Rome and events such as the demotion of Cardinal Burke[4] mean for the restoration of traditional Catholicism?

The Synod on the Family was a colossal wake-up call to the Church, to the whole body of the faithful. It showed us, in no uncertain

---

3. Fourteenth Ordinary General Assembly of the Synod of Bishops, October 4–25, 2015, on "The Vocation and Mission of the Family in the Church and in the Contemporary World."

4. On November 8, 2014, Raymond Leo Cardinal Burke was removed as Prefect of the Apostolic Signatura and named Patron of the Sovereign Military Order of Malta. This was widely interpreted as a punishment for the Cardinal's strong stance against pastoral accommodationism at the Third Extraordinary General Assembly of the Synod of Bishops, October 5–19, 2014, and for remarks he had made about poor Church leadership.

terms, that many of our shepherds are like drunks or madmen, and that we cannot sit back and take for granted that the Faith is safe. I think modern Catholics have generally been rather passive: they are trained to take what is given to them, and don't stir themselves to action very easily—let's say, to do something as easy and rewarding as studying the catechism, or more challenging like studying texts from the Fathers and Doctors of the Church. That was the problem with the reception of Vatican II and the reformed liturgy: the "experts" spoon-fed us all this stuff, and we choked it down, instead of spitting it out or demanding to see the ingredients.

But you can see to an astonishing extent that this wasn't working with the Synod. The experts tried to pull the wool over our eyes, as usual, and it failed not only among us, but even among themselves. The Machiavellians were too clever by half. It came as a resounding warning to the Church Militant. The ensuing divisions in the ranks are unfortunate but highly necessary so that the truth can be proved and the deceiver exposed. As St Paul says: "I hear that when you come together in the church, there are schisms among you; and in part I believe it. For there must be also heresies, that they also, who are approved, may be made manifest among you."[5]

In short, the Synod has galvanized many Catholics around the world to take up their catechisms and defend the Faith. This is all to the good and, in God's mercy, may portend a still greater opening of minds and hearts to traditionalism, which has been attentively clued in to the hermeneutic of rupture and discontinuity for five decades or more and which offers a coherent and convincing way out of the madness.

As for that outstanding defender of the Catholic Faith, Cardinal Burke, I am inclined to see the shift in position as a custom-made opportunity for His Eminence to become, more than ever, a world-wide ambassador for the *usus antiquior*, for the theology, spirituality, fine arts, discipline, and law that sustain it and emerge from it, and for traditional Catholic doctrine on faith and morals. I don't see this as a matter of making lemonade out of lemons. Will he not end up more active and more influential, not less? If Pope Francis

5. 1 Corinthians 11:18–19.

really wanted to "exile" him, it's a strategic blunder that will benefit us in the end. If Pope Francis felt Cardinal Burke's time in office was up (no one has lasted long at the Signatura, if you look at the records) and wanted to give him plenty of freedom of action, then that's going to benefit us, too. However you look at it, Cardinal Burke occupies the moral high ground and the cause of tradition will continue to enjoy his wise, gentle, and generous patronage.

6

Why Catholics Are So Bad at Evangelizing—And What Needs to Change

Two good friends, fellow parishioners, are having coffee and donuts after High Mass one Sunday.

Maximilian: I enjoyed Father's homily today. His explanation of the parable of the mustard seed and the yeast in the dough hit the nail on the head.

Roberto: I thought so, too. It was neat when he said it's not just the kingdom of God that can be compared to a seed or yeast, but Christ Himself, who came into our world as a tiny baby in a manger, grew up in the middle of nowhere, and died as a convicted criminal—in the world's eyes, contemptibly small. His way of gathering disciplines, His itinerant preaching—it was all like that seed, seemingly insignificant but now grown over the ages into a tree that stretches across the world.

Max: He had that quotation from Ratzinger, too—that Jesus not only preaches, inaugurates, and rules the kingdom of God, but He *is* the Kingdom, "in person." And when we receive Him in Holy Communion, then His own words are perfectly fulfilled: "The kingdom of God is within you."[1]

---

1. Luke 17:21.

Berto: And then he said the same is true for individual Catholics: *we* should be those seeds that mature into great bushes to give protection and rest to others who are weary and searching. We should be like a yeast rolled into the dough of our society, lifting it up to God.

Max: Right around that spot, he said something terribly important. Let me see if I can remember how he put it. "You know, modern Catholics are not very good at spreading the Faith. In centuries past, we had missionaries who went from one end of the earth to the other, planting the standard of the Cross, preaching the Gospel, suffering and dying for it, bringing countless souls into the Church. Why are we so timid, so unwilling to stick our necks out? Why do we hide our light under a bushel, content to keep our faith a private affair? Jesus said the kingdom *begins* like a mustard seed, but it's not supposed to *remain* there. It should grow, branch out, and get huge, changing the lives of many. The dough is supposed to rise and become delicious, nourishing bread."

Berto: And he went on to say that this doesn't seem to be happening much anymore. The Church is missionary by nature, but many live as though it's enough to be a believer, and never think of speaking a word of invitation to anyone else around them who isn't already going to church. In this way we are not growing and leavening as we should. Why aren't RCIA classes packed, standing room only? Why isn't the Easter Vigil everywhere full of baptisms, confirmations, and first communions?

Max: I've been puzzling over that for many years.

Berto: Have you gotten anywhere in your thinking? Why is evangelization practically non-existent among Catholics?

Max: Well, I'm sure there are many reasons, but I can think of at least three major ones. The first is maybe the most obvious. We—I'm speaking of people in the modern West—we have completely bought into the error of the Enlightenment that religion is a private affair and that we should not "bother" anyone else about their faith or lack of faith in God. It's "between a man and his Maker." It's just a matter of individual conscience. This comes from the fundamental error of thinking that man is not a social animal—as if his happiness, even his salvation, is purely individualistic. We're all atoms floating in the void, and besides, we can't know for sure if anything we're thinking is objectively true. So we keep our big ideas to ourselves and muddle along as best we can, acting selfishly or altruistically depending on what seems to suit the need of the hour. It's a depressing picture of human beings and their life together. It certainly doesn't recognize that man is inherently relational and religious, and that he must find his fulfillment in communal worship of the true God.

Berto: If religion is just a private affair and you can't even know for sure whether you're right or not, why would you go out of your way to talk it up with neighbors, acquaintances, coworkers? You might "offend their sensibilities."

Max: A second issue is this. Thanks to the unholy "spirit of Vatican II," we have drunk the Kool-Aid of universalism: everyone, or nearly everyone, will be saved. God is so merciful that He either sends no one to hell, or you have to work really hard to send yourself to hell—you've got to want it badly. So, basically, there's no urgency to spread the Faith, because we just assume that most people are of good will and headed in the right direction.

Berto: Your point is proved by the auto-canonization that occurs at practically every Novus Ordo funeral. Looking back on my youth, I can't think of a funeral I went to where we didn't hear about how great the deceased person was and how "he's now in a better place" and "we'll all get to see him again in heaven," etc. The Vatican doesn't need to simplify the process of canonization any further; all you need to do is die and you're in!

Max: It was the same where I grew up. I can't recall a single funeral where we focused our attention on praying for the repose of the soul of the departed. That was what struck me most about the traditional Requiem Mass when I first attended it. For all intents and purposes, it *ignores* the faithful who are there, so intense is its focus on the fate of the departed soul.

Berto: What you're saying is perfectly summed up in the "Dies irae."

Max: Now *that's* a prayer that makes you want to get on your knees and stay there a while! But let's get back to universalism. For the Church Fathers, the default assumption is that man is *lost* without faith in Christ, without His grace.

Berto: You don't have to wait until the Church Fathers. It's already there in St Paul, clear as day. Did you catch that last line of today's Epistle? Something about "turning from idols to serve the living and true God, and waiting for His Son from heaven, Jesus, Who hath delivered us from the wrath to come"[2]?

Max: Whereas in recent decades, the default assumption is that man is automatically saved unless he massively blows it.

Berto: In fact, if we start to "disturb" people about Christ and His Church and their need for faith, grace, the sacraments, and so on, we risk unsettling them and diverting them from the path on which God was already leading them home...

Max: Our intervention might even cause them to lose their salvation by explicitly rejecting Christ whom we preach to them, whereas before they were "implicitly" accepting Him! We can't do that, right?

Berto: Have you noticed how this mentality goes hand in hand with forgetting about the rights of God and His just claims on us?

Max: Not to mention His ire towards those who do not respond to His call! The Bible—in both Testaments—is full of talk about divine wrath upon sinners. The old liturgy is the same way. You'd never

2. 1 Thessalonians 1:9–10.

know anything about this stuff from the Novus Ordo and from typical Catholic homilies, and especially from funerals.

Berto: As if God had just decided to give up some of His attributes as too old-fashioned—

Max: —or more truthfully, as if some of His spokesmen had made the decision for Him. It's bad PR to be talking about vengeance, retribution, punishment, eternal death, hellfire, and so forth. As we were just saying a moment ago, no one really *deserves* these things, which makes several hundred verses of Scripture superfluous verbiage.

Berto: It's hard to believe that people who claim to be Christians, let alone Catholics, can fall for such lunacy. I suppose it comes of no longer believing in sin, original or actual.

Max: What do you mean?

Berto: I only mean that if human beings are born in sin and prone to sin, "children of wrath"[3] who are bound to be displeasing to God, then we urgently need God's help to turn our lives around and start living for *Him,* as we were created to do. We have to be *rescued,* and Christ is the only Savior. If we don't have all the marvelous aids the Church provides, especially the sacraments, we are goners.

Max: That's exactly what all the old catechisms said. That's what the old liturgy conveys, too. In the past few years I've come to see more and more how the Catholic Faith—in its consoling truths *and* its hard truths—is intricately woven into every aspect of the traditional Roman rite, and how it's as if the new liturgy is embarrassed or ashamed or scared to tell the truth, and suppresses it, glosses it over, handles it with kid gloves. You just don't get the same doctrine, and it makes a huge difference in one's spiritual life.

---

3. Ephesians 2:3.

Berto: We are so fortunate to have the traditional liturgy here at our parish! I tell you, it has pounded into me the reality of God's holiness, the gravity of sin, and the real priorities of life.

Max: I know what you're talking about. As a Catholic growing up in a typical parish, I never even dreamed of wanting to become a "saint." That kind of talk would have made me laugh, if anyone had ever said it. Now, I *get* it. I see that this is it, the whole adventure of life, the meaning of it all.

Berto: And, as our pastor's introduced over the years Sunday Vespers, Confession in the old rite, Nuptial Masses and Requiem Masses, all of it, I've found myself *falling in love* with my faith. Can you imagine? I used to be just going through the motions, or more focused on seeing my friends—I like seeing my friends, don't get me wrong—but God is really at the center of everything. Traditional Catholicism makes you *feel* it, see it, hear it.

Max: You even *smell* it when those acolytes get going with the incense!

Berto: But we are getting a bit sidetracked. You spoke about three reasons for the lameness of Catholic evangelization. What's the third?

Max: It's simply this. There has been and still is so much doctrinal and moral confusion in the postconciliar Church that it is becoming more and more difficult for people, whether on the inside or on the outside, to know what the Church *actually teaches* and how we are supposed to live it day to day. How can you preach a Gospel when you doubt or downplay or quarrel over half of what it says? How can you preach a consistent message if you're constantly tinkering with your catechism or your liturgy?

Berto: Sadly, you're right. Ask a sampling of Catholics about the Real Presence or whether the Mass is a sacrifice. Ask them if contraception's okay, or abortion. You'll get all sorts of incoherent, contradictory answers.

Max: How can anyone with half a brain take Catholicism seriously when it permits today what it outlawed yesterday, or vice versa? When it denigrates today what it proudly hailed in the past, and promotes ideas and practices that would have churned the stomachs of countless saints? When it now treats as intolerable the pious beliefs and customs that Catholics used to follow, sometimes for a thousand years or more?

Berto: I hear what you're saying, but we have to recognize, don't we, that all this stuff is *not* Catholicism—it is only the mental fever and fog of the people running the show, and that's not the same thing at all.

Max: No, of course not, but I'm talking about the popular perception of confusion—of a Church running around in circles to play catch-up with the contemporary world. Think of the feminism and sexual liberalism, the environmentalism, the campaign against capital punishment, and what not. The advocacy of the United Nations. The Vatican's invitations to pro-abortion and pro-euthanasia speakers. It goes on and on. No wonder even those who want to be faithful Catholics are getting totally confused. At the end of the day, it looks increasingly as if you can believe anything you want and still call yourself a "Catholic."

Berto: That's not entirely true—you're not allowed to be *traditional*, that's beyond the pale. But everything else is fair game.

Max: Ah, well, such is life in the Church today. But anyway, regardless of whose fault the confusion is, how far back we trace it, or how much the Council is responsible for it, the practical effect is clear. As St Paul said: "If the trumpet give an uncertain sound, who shall prepare himself to the battle?"[4] No one rallies to a confused army, no one marches to an irregular drummer. It's as if Catholicism is a "process," morphing with the world around it, instead of a firm foundation we can build on.

4. 1 Corinthians 14:8.

Berto: I'd agree with that. (*Pauses.*) But I wonder…

Max: About what?

Berto: Your three reasons are very much to the point, but I think we need to bring in a fourth one as well.

Max: Which is…?

Berto: Let's say we *do* convince someone to listen to us, and we get them to see that Catholicism *is* a consistent belief system that gives meaning to life. What are we inviting them to, if they decide to check us out? We are spoiled at this parish with the High Mass, the beautiful sacred music, the orthodox preaching, the altar server guild, and so on, but frankly, this is one in a thousand, a diamond in a heap of coals.

Max: You're saying, if we overcome the other factors, there's still all the byproducts of the liturgical revolution to deal with—the abuses and novelties in the Mass, the banality of the music, the ugliness of so many churches…

Berto: Right. And these are a formidable obstacle to people searching for the one true religion. Surely this religion, above all, should be characterized by the beauty and splendor of its worship, an atmosphere of mystery and prayer, an intense confrontation with the supernatural. This is why the traditional worship of the Church used to be the cause of so many conversions. It was the living and breathing animal, compared to which all other religions were like shadows or cartoon sketches.

Max: Indeed, though it pains me to say it, the new Catholic worship itself is like a shadow or a cartoon of the old.

Berto: At least the old worship is still attracting converts in a place like this.

Max: Thanks be to God for that. His grace is never lacking for those who truly seek Him.

Berto: But you know how it is: the entire infrastructure is against us. We can't help looking like extremists to the outside world and to our fellow Catholics, because everyone else is so far gone in the other direction. They call us "rigid fundamentalists" and things like that.

Max: And I think one could connect a related point to yours: there is almost nothing *demanding* about being a Catholic nowadays. Fasting is mostly gone; abstinence is no longer required; the precepts of the Church are unknown or ignored; sexual discipline is passed over glibly. Why would anyone looking for a tried-and-true way of life— the "people of good will" we are supposed to be spreading the Faith to—buy into this charade? Almost all of the false religions demand more. Catholicism used to demand of us *everything*—and it promised us everything! It gave meaning to one's entire life. It permeated the day, the week, the month, the year, with signs of the sacred. It asked us to sacrifice good things for even better things. It offered us a narrow path to holiness and heaven, in the company of Our Lord, Our Lady, and a host of saints. Where is all that now?

Berto: Sure, we try to live it among ourselves as best we can, and we know it's the truth, but it is not the institutional norm any more— indeed, the all-too-human institution largely rejects it.

Max: No wonder Islam is the fastest-growing religion in the West. It takes God and religion seriously.

Berto: And we will have to do that too, if we ever expect to be mustard seeds or leaven again. It goes back to what we heard Father preach about on the last Sunday of October: we have to make Christ King of *everything*—our hearts, souls, and minds, our families, our cities and nations.

Max: Dare I say, of our Church, too?

Berto: That goes without saying.

Max (*after a pause*): We've made quite a big circuit in this conversation, haven't we?

Berto: Shall we try to sum it up so we can remember it better?

Max: Sure. The Church, and individual Catholics in it, are supposed to be mustard seeds and leaven in this world. Or, as some prefer to say, "salt and light." We have a missionary imperative from Christ to convert the world. But there are at least five serious obstacles to evangelizing today, any one of which alone would deal a serious blow to the endeavor. First, the privatization of religion. Second, the rejection of original sin and the assumption of universal salvation. Third, the widespread doctrinal and moral confusion in the Church. Fourth, the banality and irreverence of mainstream Catholic worship. Fifth, the utter lack of ascetical demands. When you put all these together, you get Catholics who don't think they should bother other people about religion, who assume that most people are already fine, who are not even quite sure they know what they believe, have nothing especially attractive to invite people to, and are not living and promoting a way of life that would respond to the needs of any serious searcher.

Berto: So, let me guess at a grand conclusion. You're saying that all this "New Evangelization" rhetoric is pretty much hot air? And that it can't possibly work?

Max: Yes, that's right. It's premised on the assumption that basically "all is well" inside the Church, and we just need to "invite" and "welcome" people to "share" the love feast with us. As Ratzinger once said, it's the dead burying the dead and calling it renewal.

Berto: Or to put it more sharply: where there is novelty, there is disease and death; where there is tradition, there is health and new life.

Max: What we actually need is—

Berto: —let me guess again: *Old* Evangelization.

Max: Spot on. The stuff the saints used to do. The way they converted the entire world to the Faith once upon a time. That's what we have to do today: *real* worship, *real* doctrine, *real* morals, *real* demands. Unadulterated dogma, the imitation of Christ in our moral life, and, above all, participation in the sacred liturgy. Then the Lord will bless us with real results.

Berto: And that's why, as we've often said to other parishioners, no one should be embarrassed to invite friends, family, even strangers, to join us for High Mass. Who knows what seed it might plant, whose heart it could touch in a new and deeper way?

Max: All the more because we can't expect any knights in shining armor to ride in to our aid. We've got to do the Lord's work and go out into the vineyard or else no one will. And there's no time to waste...

Berto: Oh my, look at the time! I have to get going—we've got company coming over for dinner and I promised my wife that I'd prepare the main course. She's cooking all week long, and home-schooling our kids on top of it...

Max: You and your wife *are* doing the Lord's work, that's for sure! God bless you both. Thanks for the good conversation.

Berto: I'll give you a call later in the week. Pray for me.

Max: I will. And you for me.

7

"A Deeply Felt Hunger and Thirst for the Unequivocally Sacred"

An Interview with Andrej Kutarna

How did you come to the "Mass of the Ages"?

My journey into the traditional liturgy was gentle and gradual. I grew up in a very typical suburban American parish and sang in its children's choir and, later, adult choir. The liturgy was very "contemporary" in style, but I didn't know that at the time, not having anything else to compare it with.

In high school two things happened: I got involved in a charismatic prayer group, which re-animated my faith, and I took a course in philosophy that brought me into contact with Plato, Aristotle, Augustine, and Aquinas. After a couple of years, my interest in the charismatic prayer group waned, but my intellectual life soared. I began to study theology, too, and had a vague longing for a form of prayer and liturgy that would correspond to the depth and breadth of philosophy and theology. Without knowing it, I was searching for the traditional worship of the Church, which was born of the ancient Fathers, developed by the medievals, and faithfully handed down to us from Trent onwards.

I was fortunate to attend a college[1] where the "Ordinary Form" of the Mass was celebrated always in Latin and with Gregorian chant. This pleased me very much because it seemed like what I had been looking for. But then, towards the end of my four years there, I had

---

1. Thomas Aquinas College in California.

several opportunities to attend Tridentine "low Masses" and the occasional sung Mass in a small chapel. The intensity of silence, the palpable holiness, the richness of the prayers, gripped me powerfully.

When I went on to graduate school at the Catholic University of America, I made a priority of finding out where this glorious Mass was celebrated in Washington, D.C., and ended up at Old St Mary's, where I experienced a *Missa cantata* with full ceremonial. I felt I had finally "come home" as a Catholic: this was the point of arrival, what I had been searching for. That was over 20 years ago, and I have never wavered in this conviction. I fell in love and I am still in love—it's like a good marriage!

You are a lecturer in philosophy, a composer and conductor of sacred music, and a passionate writer about liturgy. Some people may regard this as a very broad variety of subjects. How would you describe the connection between them?

I learned early on that these different subjects complement and almost demand one another. As time went on, I discovered so many great minds in the Western tradition from antiquity to modernity who recognized a deep connection between music, philosophy, religion, and life—just think of Plato and Aristotle, Boethius and Augustine, Schopenhauer and Nietzsche, Pieper and Ratzinger.

When I was first studying philosophy, I had a nagging sense that moderns were neglecting the religious dimension of ancient thought, and then I discovered the work of Pierre Hadot and others, who showed that philosophy is always rooted in a primordial religious quest and in traditional practices of *askesis*, and that it culminates in a mystical ascent to the Good. This, of course, is the natural disposition for supernatural grace. The Incarnation is God's answer to the fundamental question posed by our very humanity in all its marvelous distinctness and potentiality.

St Clement of Alexandria says that Christ is the New Song, the *Logos* taking flesh as a hymn of creation in which we can all join. Music is speech elevated, exultant; through singing, what might be a mere truth (say, a sentence of Scripture or of the liturgy) is elevated to praise, homage, glory. In this way, I see an internal sequence: the examination of human nature and the world gives rise to philosophy; philosophy pursued with honesty and zeal gives rise to the desire for worship of the Transcendent; this worship in its perfection is liturgical and musical. To me, these subjects are a continuum.

What was "first"—did liturgy lead you to music or was it the other way round?

My experience of the liturgy was always connected with music, even when the quality of the music happened to be poor. So I had a deep sense that these two things naturally went together. Thanks to Ratzinger, I now understand much better *why* this is true, but in order to have that sense, one first needs to be immersed in the phenomena.

A huge turning point for me was discovering Gregorian chant at the end of high school. A music teacher gave me a *Graduale Romanum* from the 1940's, and I was fascinated by the strange neumes and the texts, neither of which I could read, which provoked me to try to learn how to do so. In college, I took Latin (it was a required subject) and joined a chant schola. Singing the proper chants each week at Mass—in the Novus Ordo, mind you!—I fell in love with their beauty, subtlety, and piety. This "musical conversion" paralleled my discovery that liturgy could and *should* be celebrated in a way that was theocentric and vertical, rather than anthropocentric and horizontal. And, of course, it paved the way for my discovery of the traditional Mass, which is God-oriented through and through, saturated with the piety of centuries of Christian tradition.

Now to your book. The title—both in English[2] and in Czech[3]—suggests that the Church is in some sort of crisis. Could you describe where you think the root of this crisis lies?

There are many aspects of the crisis, needless to say, and it is not always easy to make a diagnosis of the root problem, particularly as

2. *Resurgent in the Midst of Crisis.*
3. *Povstávání z prachu.*

it may differ from one area of the Church to another (what may be true of Europe and North America may not be the same in Africa or in Asia). But I think we can be confident of the correctness of Joseph Ratzinger's judgment: "I am convinced that the crisis in the Church that we are experiencing today is to a large extent due to the disintegration of the liturgy."[4] This is a judgment shared by Cardinal Burke, Cardinal Cañizares-Llovera, Cardinal Sarah, and many other astute observers of our times.

In our rush to dialogue with the world, in our accommodation of the ideas (and idols) of modernity, and in our embrace of pastoral activism, we have forgotten the primacy of God, the primacy of liturgical prayer, the primacy of tradition, and the primacy of grace. This is a fatal blow to the Church in her human element. After all, Our Lord promised that the gates of hell would not prevail against *the Church,* which means that *somewhere* she will always survive until the Second Coming of Christ. He never promised that any *local* church would survive—and just as Islam wiped out Christianity in Africa and Asia Minor in ancient times, so the spirit of compromise with modernity has been wiping out Christianity in the Western world of today. There will always be pockets of faithful Catholics who hold fast to orthodoxy, which means both "right doctrine" and "right worship." But that there is a crisis of faith, and that this crisis has been precipitated by the poor decisions and the faulty philosophy of the ecclesiastical hierarchy over the past half-century, only a man deaf and blind could deny.

In the countries behind the Iron Curtain we maybe haven't experienced the post-conciliar liturgical mess to such an extent as in Western Europe or the U.S. Do you think the usus antiquior *may be important even in our liturgically rather conservative context?*

I would say two things in response to the question.

First, it is becoming more and more known that the liturgical reform operated on the basis of radical principles, which found their way into the resulting liturgical books. One example is the

___
4. *Milestones,* 148.

manner in which the redactors of the Missal systematically removed or downplayed asceticism and the theme of *contemptus mundi*[5] that is so much a part of Catholic spirituality; another example is the introduction of new Eucharistic anaphoras in the Roman Rite, even though for over 1,500 years it had only a single one, the ancient and venerable Roman Canon. "Difficult" passages of Scripture that had been read for as many centuries as we have records were suppressed. There were also deformations in the Divine Office, such as the abandonment of the weekly *cursus*, the omission of "difficult" psalm verses, and serious meddling with the texts of the hymns. Such things are startling innovations and monumental ruptures with longstanding tradition; they are serious issues, regardless of whether or not the *ars celebrandi* is reverent and respectful of rubrics and texts.

Second, it is only a matter of time before the liturgical liberalism of other "more advanced" nations negatively affects Eastern Europe. We see how political, economic, and cultural liberalism have already begun to colonize Eastern Europe. The same will happen with liturgical abuses, novelties, and heresies. For instance, Poland, one of the few nations to have stood strong against the abuse of communion in the hand, finally capitulated in 2005, surely due to ongoing pressure from "the liturgical establishment." It is therefore urgently necessary to rediscover our Catholic tradition and to do so from its pure and fresh sources.

Many people, even priests and bishops, seem to think that the popularity of the traditional Latin Mass is just a temporary fad among the younger generation, a fad driven by some kind of fear of the complexity of life in the postmodern era. Why do you disagree?

If I may cite Pope Benedict XVI once more: "What earlier generations held as sacred, remains sacred and great for us, too.... It behooves all of us to preserve the riches which have developed in the Church's faith and prayer, and to give them their proper place."[6]

---

5. Contempt of the world.
6. Letter to Bishops, July 7, 2007.

Human nature in its essence does not change; the natural symbols used by religion (fire, water, incense, gold, elevated places, facing east, etc.) do not change; our need for churches, vessels, vestments, and furnishings that are special, splendid, numinous, "out of the ordinary," does not change.

If anything, modern man is *more* in need of the prayers and practices of traditional Catholicism, because he is in very great danger of forgetting his dependence on God, on the natural world, and on tradition. We would not exist without God; we cannot live well unless we have a proper relationship to creation; and Christianity could not exist without tradition. The reality of God, the honor and glory due to Him, the right use and destination of created goods, and the fullness of Christian tradition—all of these are found, harmoniously *and* provocatively, in the traditional liturgies of the Church, both Eastern and Western.

It is not fear that drives the traditionalist, but love of excellence and hatred of banality. It is not a fad but a deeply felt hunger and thirst for the unequivocally sacred. God Himself is the source of this hunger and thirst, and He will never stop causing it among the faithful.

In the first chapter of your book you state that the traditional Mass is the ultimate "children's Mass." Why do you think so?

For me, it's a simple thing. If you have a boring liturgy with a lot of people talking all the time and nothing special happening, nothing interesting to look at or listen to, children will be bored. If you have the awesome sound of the pipe organ, the mysterious melodies of the chant, the archaic majesty of the Latin tongue, the swinging of censers with billowing clouds of smoke, elaborate chasubles and copes passing in procession or solemnly facing the high altar and its tabernacle, ministers caught up in a sacred choreography, a whole church hushed in silence for the great Canon, and so forth, what child would not pay attention, come under the sway of this symphony of symbols, get caught up in its transcendent motion, and be slowly, permanently formed in a Catholic imagination and sensibility?

It does not matter if a child fully understands it or not—none of us fully understands the divine! The liturgy should be a kind of infinite expanse that one never reaches the end of, to match the human soul's capacity for the infinite. If worship is excessively tailored to us, to our everyday mode of operation, it will quickly lose its efficacy, and people will cease to be Catholic.

Many Catholics who are looking for an alternative to the Novus Ordo often frequent the Divine Liturgies of Eastern Catholic churches. You have some experience in this regard. How would you describe the principal difference in emphasis between the classical Roman rite and the Eastern liturgies?

You are right: I love the Divine Liturgy of St John Chrysostom and have attended it regularly over many years. The Eastern liturgies in general are more vocally participative, extroverted, joyous, and centered on the Resurrection, while Western liturgies incorporate more silence and more singing by scholas, are more "interior" in their manner, and focus more on the mystery of the Passion of Our Lord.

Having said this, one mustn't forget how much the great historic liturgies have in common, in their texts (think of the constant doxologizing), their "ethos" of solemnity, their embrace of the beauty of traditional music and architecture, and their great sensitivity to the symbolic value of every word and gesture (nothing is left to spontaneity or extemporaneity). In this sense, I find that attending a Byzantine liturgy, even one in English with a lot of congregational singing, is much more like attending a Tridentine High Mass than it is like attending a Novus Ordo Mass. The rich prayers, the formal attitude, the solemn ceremonial, give to both Eastern and Western rites the same ancient and therefore timeless "feel."

Is the traditional Latin Mass the only way out of this crisis—the only way to the renewal of the Church?

A widespread restoration of the traditional Latin liturgy would, in fact, strongly reverse the trends of secularization, relativism, indifferentism, and modernism that are ravaging the Church. But there is also no doubt that people abandon the practice of the Faith for many reasons, and insipid, uninspiring liturgy is only one of them. Conversely, good liturgy is not the only thing necessary; we need good preaching, sound catechesis, robust social fellowship and support, the pursuit of spiritual and corporal works of mercy. But if the liturgy is done badly, nothing else will work, either. It is part of the divine economy: "Seek first the kingdom of God and His righteousness, and all these other things will be given to you as well."[7]

In an ideal world without the likes of Archbishop Bugnini, how do you imagine the liturgical recommendations of Sacrosanctum Concilium, *and Vatican II more broadly, could or should have been implemented?*

In retrospect, I think we are in a better position to see that some of what got into the documents of the Second Vatican Council reflected the ephemeral enthusiasm of the 1960's, which is now very dated.

The Constitution on the Liturgy lays down general theological principles that have permanent validity but goes on to propose many particular changes, which are not doctrinal matters but disciplinary and therefore prudential in nature. Looking back, we can ask whether, for example, the suppression of the office of Prime was really necessary; whether so-called "useless repetition" is really so useless after all; whether the Church calendar really needed anything more than superficial refinements, as opposed to a massive overhaul. In other words, many pages of this Constitution have not aged well and are a bit embarrassing now to look at; they are better forgotten, along with much else from the 1960's. Indeed, it seems to me that the way forward is to get beyond the insistence on the 1962 missal (which, admittedly, serves as a necessary reference point) and return to a healthier stage of the rite, namely, as it was found in 1948, before experts began to meddle with the substance of it.

On the other hand, this much seems clear: the call for a fuller *participatio actuosa,* which is not an invention of Vatican II but a *desideratum* of St Pius X, has still not been achieved in most traditional Catholic communities, inasmuch as the people do not sing—or

7. Matthew 6:33.

worse, are discouraged from singing—the Ordinary of the Mass in Gregorian chant. Moreover, the Propers of the Mass are frequently not chanted, either because they are replaced with psalm tones and motets, or because the Low Mass is taken as the norm rather than the Sung Mass. In my opinion, these are serious deficiencies that need to be addressed over time in the traditional milieu.

How can a lay person without a nearby Latin Mass community join in the renewal as you propose it in the book?

The first thing I would recommend is to adopt some part of the traditional Divine Office for personal recitation. The Divine Office, too, is part of the public liturgy of the Church, and when we pray it, we are uniting ourselves to the prayer of Jesus Christ and His Mystical Body. One could start modestly with Prime and Compline; those who have more time could do Lauds and Vespers.

As a Benedictine oblate and a layman, I appreciate the "bread and butter" spirituality of the monks: in addition to the Divine Office, doing some *lectio divina* or prayerful reading of Scripture, or reading a good book by a Father or Doctor of the Church. All of this is part of the forgotten treasury of the Church and is therefore an important component of the renewal.

As a teacher, I am a huge advocate of ongoing education. People need to read good books about dogma, the liturgy, the saints, and spread these books among their friends. Magazines and blogs can be helpful, too, in this regard, as long as they do not take the place of reading books (especially the Bible, the Missal, the Divine Office).

Above all, I would say that even a person who lives far from a community where the *usus antiquior* is celebrated should do his best to get to a traditional Mass at least once in a while, to "recharge the batteries," so to speak. In my life there have been times when, due to vacation schedules, the old Mass has been unavailable for months at a time. I have always been amazed at how a single Mass during such a period can be like an oasis in a desert. Yes, it's painful to be reminded of what one normally lacks, but it is also a blessing, a consolation, an opportunity to renew one's commitment to Christ, His Church, and Catholic tradition.

8

The Papacy: In Service
of Sacred Tradition

Brother Barsanuphius: Good morning, Brother. To my surprise, the guest house is completely ready for today's arrivals, and we have some time before the next office. Are you free for a conversation? We could pick up where we left off.

Brother Romuald: That would be an excellent thing to do. Let's sit over here by the herb garden.

Br. Barsanuphius: My problem comes down to the relationship between the "conservative" instinct of submitting oneself to the pope, and the "traditionalist" instinct of taking tradition as a safe guide and making a yardstick of it. I see, on the one hand, that the instinct of revering the pope and going along with his teaching is healthy, but on other hand, I know enough of Church history to see that this is not foolproof. And besides, what is meant by "the pope's teaching" is far from simple, since it is not a uniform body of teaching but comes in various forms and degrees of authority.

Br. Romuald: It's so like you to get right to the heart of the matter! But what could ever be the problem with taking tradition as our pole star?

Br. Barsanuphius: Some people see "tradition" as an intellectual construct that can never be determinate, so appealing to it encourages, they think, an almost Protestant spirit of "private judgment."

Br. Romuald: But as other people see it, the approach of submitting oneself to the pope can go wrong if it places too much weight, in an ultramontanist spirit, on the *dicta et facta*, the words and actions, of the reigning pontiff.

Br. Barsanuphius: That's the contrast in a nutshell.

Br. Romuald: Perhaps both of these positions are extremes. Isn't there a genuine *via media* that holds to the real primacy of the pope as well as to the normative standing of the tradition he is called to serve—and which he can betray in one way or another?

Br. Barsanuphius: Yes, exactly! I used to think that a pope could never say or do anything wrong at all, as if it's his job to be a sort of Delphic oracle who always gives an inspired answer, or a God-king whom we all venerate—"the Great Leader" in an almost Communist or fascist way.

Br. Romuald: You were suffering from a common illusion among Catholics. Most do not grasp well the meaning and the role of the papacy.

Br. Barsanuphius: Right. It was a watershed moment for me when I found no less than Joseph Ratzinger saying in *The Spirit of the Liturgy*—let me see, I have this book in my satchel... Ah yes, here it is:

> After the Second Vatican Council, the impression arose that the pope really could do anything in liturgical matters, especially if he were acting on the mandate of an ecumenical council. Eventually, the idea of the givenness of the liturgy, the fact that one cannot do with it what one will, faded from the public consciousness of the West. In fact, the First Vatican Council had in no way defined the pope as an absolute monarch. On the contrary, it presented him as the guarantor of obedience to the revealed Word. The pope's authority is bound to the tradition of faith, and that also applies to the liturgy. It is not "manufactured" by the authorities. Even the pope can only be a humble servant of its lawful development and

abiding integrity and identity. . . . The authority of the pope is not unlimited; it is at the service of Sacred Tradition.[1]

Br. Romuald: A fine passage indeed, and indicative of a deep trend in his thinking. For if I'm not mistaken, he reiterated this position as pope in 2005.

Br. Barsanuphius: You're right. I have it printed on a sheet of paper tucked into this book, because it seemed so important to me:

> The power that Christ conferred upon Peter and his Successors is, in an absolute sense, a mandate to serve. The power of teaching in the Church involves a commitment to the service of obedience to the faith. The pope is not an absolute monarch whose thoughts and desires are law. On the contrary: the pope's ministry is a guarantee of obedience to Christ and to his Word. He must not proclaim his own ideas, but rather constantly bind himself and the Church to obedience to God's Word, in the face of every attempt to adapt it or water it down, and every form of opportunism. . . . The pope knows that in his important decisions, he is bound to the great community of faith of all times, to the binding interpretations that have developed throughout the Church's pilgrimage. Thus, his power is not being above the Word of God, but at the service of it. It is incumbent upon him to ensure that this Word continues to be present in its greatness and to resound in its purity, so that it is not torn to pieces by continuous changes in usage.[2]

Br. Romuald: Well, then, we seem to be in agreement about the actual role of the pope and the limitations of his office. But I recall that yesterday you were struggling with the problem of John Henry Newman's conversion and how, in a way, he switched his allegiance from an abstract construct called "tradition" to a concrete standard called "papacy."[3]

---

1. Joseph Ratzinger, *The Spirit of the Liturgy*, trans. John Saward (San Francisco: Ignatius Press, 2000), 165–66.
2. Pope Benedict XVI, Homily at the Mass of the Possession of the Chair of the Bishop of Rome, Basilica of St John Lateran, May 7, 2005.
3. On the development of Newman's understanding of papal infallibility, including the role of the papacy in his ecclesiology and his anxieties about possible

Br. Barsanuphius: Yes. In 1840, Newman believed that "Tradition = Catholicism," while in 1845 he had come to believe that "Pope = Catholicism." *Ubi Petrus, ibi ecclesia.*[4]

Br. Romuald: In light of the foregoing quotations from Ratzinger, however, wouldn't we have to maintain that the difference between Newman the Anglican and Newman the Catholic is not this at all, but rather that by 1845 he had come to see that the pope is an integral and central part of the picture, as the one who *can* determine and define—and indeed *has* historically determined and defined—what is and is not according to Tradition, or what is or is not taught in Scripture?

Br. Barsanuphius: Of course. The absence of this magisterial power in Protestantism explains why it exists in over 30,000 denominations. Someone has to be able to say, when push comes to shove, what is or is not taught by Scripture and Tradition.

Br. Romuald: Surely, the next step is to say that the pope cannot in any way add to or subtract from the dual font of Revelation, namely Scripture and Tradition. The Magisterium *interprets* Revelation; it does not originate or modify it. The Magisterium is decisively secondary to it. To hold this more modest view of the Magisterium is pure Catholicism, without a whiff of 1840's Anglicanism. One may and must view the head of the Church on earth as a visible sign and source of communion within the Church without viewing his authority as absolute over doctrine and discipline.

Br. Barsanuphius: How could I disagree? This seems like pure common sense to me. But how do we know when a pope is acting according to his office and when he might be departing from it? If he is *ultra vires*, outside the bounds—can we ever know that?

---

misinterpretations of Vatican I, see Frances A. Sullivan, SJ, "Newman on Infallibility," in *Newman After a Hundred Years,* ed. Ian Ker and Alan G. Hill (Oxford: Oxford University Press, 1990), 419–46.

4. Where Peter is, there is the Church.

Br. Romuald: We *must* be able to know that. At least *something* of the content of Revelation can be known by faithful Catholics with such certitude that if a pope *were* to contradict it, they could *know* he was in error and refuse to follow the error, in spite of its papal patronage.

Br. Barsanuphius: If one were to deny that the orthodox faith could be known *at all* apart from the teaching of the current incumbent of the papacy, how would that be any different from epistemological skepticism about the knowability, objectivity, constancy, and universality of the Catholic Faith?

Br. Romuald: Indeed—we would not even be able to recognize the continuity of the Faith over time, since whatever continuity showed up in the historical record would be merely the result of a lot of popes who happened to will the same thing. It would not be a guarantee that what they adhered to was the truth and that they would never adhere to anything different.

Br. Barsanuphius: Such an approach would negate the age-old rule of St Vincent of Lérins, who taught that we must adhere to doctrines believed "always, everywhere, and by everyone."[5]

Br. Romuald: Exactly! My dear brother, you surely see by now that we cannot sidestep or wave away the need for rational criteria to determine how and when to obey the pope or embrace his statements, precisely in order to remain faithful ourselves to the immutable truths of the Faith. By this, I mean that no matter how much our insights into God may develop over time, they will never contradict that which has been solemnly or consistently taught before.

Br. Barsanuphius: As you were explaining to me last week, this is the reason why John of St Thomas, Cajetan, Bellarmine, Melchior Cano, and other great theologians of the past wrote extensively on

---

5. St Vincent of Lérins, *Commonitory for the Antiquity and Universality of the Catholic Faith Against the Profane Novelties of All Heresies*, ch. 2.

these matters, distinguishing carefully between papal statements or judgments that must be accepted, and those that might be questioned or, in dire cases, must be rejected.

Br. Romuald: Perhaps we should not speak so hypothetically. Many things said and done by more recent popes are extremely hard to reconcile with the manifest teaching of earlier councils and popes and even Sacred Scripture; it's downright scandalous at times. Simply compare the encyclical letter *Casti Connubii* to the apostolic exhortation *Amoris Laetitia*!

Br. Barsanuphius: Ah, brother, you have raised a painful subject. For quite some time, to be honest, I've avoided following Vatican news, so as not to lose heart or become angry.

Br. Romuald: I totally sympathize with the desire not to know how bad things have become, but we must recognize that the issues at stake—such as the proposal that we should invite to Holy Communion those who are living objectively in a state of adultery—concern the very *essence* of our Faith. We cannot ignore them, wishing they would go away.

Br. Barsanuphius: Besides, people will be asking us what our opinion is. As men of religion, we have a duty to be well-informed and well-educated—

Br. Romuald: —and prepared for those awkward moments after Mass or in the gift shop.

Br. Barsanuphius: You can say that again! A few weeks ago, when I was running the shop, a man came in and started going on about how the situation in the Church today was so bad that it was surely a sign that we did not have a legitimate pope. I tried to reason with him about the difference between not having a pope at all and having a bad pope. If you've got a bad pope, you can explain the desperate situation in the Church without much difficulty. In this case, we apply Ockham's razor.

Br. Romuald: Did you convince him?

Br. Barsanuphius: I think so. I told him that our situation would never get any better unless he was praying every day for the pope and the Church—and made sure to protect himself against evil spirits. After friendly banter and a cup of tea, he bought a bunch of St Benedict medals, a few rosaries, and a small booklet with Prime and Compline, and left in good spirits.

Br. Romuald: Good to hear. What a blessing that gift shop is.

Br. Barsanuphius: But the conversation made me melancholy. In fact, it's what prompted our own conversation yesterday about the insistence of traditionalists that the Church's teaching in the past—for example, the decrees, canons, and anathemas of the Council of Trent—is a permanent standard for, and measure of, the present and the future. And then one is tempted to doubt oneself. A voice whispers in one's ear: "Aren't you too attached to past glories and certainties?"

Br. Romuald: We can all feel that way at times. Yet the past is given to us as the foundation on which the present is built, and we do not tamper with the foundation under a building unless we want it to fall down.

Br. Barsanuphius: A sign that we are not crazy is the not-insignificant number of priests, bishops, and cardinals around the world who are shocked and sickened by what they see happening in Rome. This is not at all about distrust of the pope, rejection of the papacy, or the exaltation of private judgment. It is about distrust of those who are damaging the Church and the Faith their predecessors taught.

Br. Romuald: Positively, it is about holding fast to the teaching of Our Lord in the Gospels about marriage and divorce—teaching clearly stated and determined past all doubt by the Magisterium of the Church, including most recently (and repeatedly) by John Paul II and Benedict XVI.

Br. Barsanuphius: Amen to that. What is the pope *for*, if not to guard and proclaim the Deposit of Faith, integral and unadulterated?

Br. Romuald: And to think this used to be taken for granted! Newman calls the pope a *remora*, "a breakwater, a hindrance, a stopper against innovation," as the genial Father Hunwicke puts it.[6] By his very office the pope is to be stubbornly conservative, doctrinally unoriginal, utterly traditional.

Br. Barsanuphius: That is what the Roman Church was famous for in the first millennium of Christianity—her Roman Canon is the most ancient and unchanged of all anaphoras—and she largely retained that role in the second millennium as well.

Br. Romuald: One of my favorite examples of how much the Roman Church resisted change is that it did not even recite the Creed during Mass for many centuries, since that was not a part of the existing liturgy, and finally incorporated it only after everyone was using it elsewhere.[7]

Br. Barsanuphius: We sure could have used some of that spirit of resistance to change in the sixties and seventies, when secular culture had more or less made a religion out of evolution!

Br. Romuald: You can say that again.

Br. Barsanuphius: Clearly, what we need is a reforming pope, a man like St Gregory VII, St Pius V, or St Pius X, one who can come in and be that stopper against innovation—with, I might as well say it, a pair of strong arms to sweep out the Augean stables.

Br. Romuald: What's strange beyond belief is that there are people out there who would think we are disloyal Catholics for saying such things. How little they know of loyalty *or* Catholicism!

6. Fr John Hunwicke, "Pope or Tradition?," at the blog *Fr Hunwicke's Mutual Enrichment,* January 5, 2015.

7. Jungmann, *Mass of the Roman Rite,* 1:467–70.

Br. Barsanuphius: In any case, by God's grace I will never abandon Our Lord or the See of Peter or the Catholic Faith that has been handed down to each generation in the official doctrine of the Church. As the first pope said: "To whom shall we go? You have the words of eternal life."[8]

Br. Romuald: Well said—even if we may be legitimately perplexed and grieved by the latest successor of Peter, to whom Our Lord, were He still walking the paths of this earth, would have plenty of reason to utter the same words as he did to the first pope: "Get behind me, Satan: you are thinking the thoughts of men, and not the thoughts of God."[9]

Br. Barsanuphius: "The thoughts of men, and not the thoughts of God…" That reminds me. Did you hear the news about the Buenos Aires letter being put into the *Acta Apostolicae Sedis*?

Br. Romuald: Alas, yes. What do you make of it?

Br. Barsanuphius: As far as what the texts *say*, it's nothing new. Astute observers all along have known that sacramental access for Catholics living in adultery is what both Synods as well as *Amoris Laetitia* have always been angling towards. Conservatives who kept doing hermeneutical somersaults to prove that "nothing has changed" now have enough egg on their face for a lifetime supply of omelettes. The defenders of continuity have just been unceremoniously dumped, while the agents of revolution have received the signal: "full steam ahead."

Br. Romuald: But it raises the stakes, doesn't it, invoking "magisterial authority" and sticking it in the *Acta* and so forth?

Br. Barsanuphius: It seems to be a favorite move nowadays to think that slapping the label "magisterial" onto a package will suddenly

8. John 6:68.
9. Matthew 16:23.

93

make the contents edible or even healthy. No, *that* depends on the ingredients, not on the label.

Br. Romuald: But it seems that including something in the *Acta* is a big deal. I remember reading in a neoscholastic manual from the fifties a statement that "whatever appears in the acts of the Holy See may be assumed to be binding teaching, since there is no more official manner in which to publish documents intended to bind the faithful with a religious submission of will and intellect."

Br. Barsanuphius: For one thing, you are forgetting your *Lumen Gentium*.

Br. Romuald: There are some things I have never tried very hard to remember.

Br. Barsanuphius: Come now, this document is your friend—on this point, at least. It says that one must gauge authoritative statements by many criteria: the type of document in question, the repetition of a doctrine, the clear intention to define or condemn.[10] Although published in the *Acta*, this recent thing is just a letter to a small group of bishops, not even an episcopal conference; it enunciates a novelty rather than repeating what has always been taught; and it is not couched in language that could possibly vie with Canon 915,[11] which expresses either dominical teaching or a conclusion logically derived from dominical teaching.

Br. Romuald: In short, it changes nothing in the Church's doctrine or discipline.

Br. Barsanuphius: Nor *could* it, for that matter. It's a bit like saying,

10. See Second Vatican Council, Dogmatic Constitution on the Church *Lumen Gentium* (November 21, 1964), n. 25.
11. Canon 915 of the 1983 *Code of Canon Law* reads: "Those who have been excommunicated or interdicted after the imposition or declaration of the penalty and others obstinately persevering in manifest grave sin are not to be admitted to holy communion."

"There are special circumstances in which it might be helpful to square a circle." But a circle can never be squared. Therefore the special circumstances will never arise.

Br. Romuald: Well said.

Br. Barsanuphius: Getting back to your manual, let us be frank: the neoscholastic manuals have their strengths, but a sane, moderate account of papal authority is not one of them. Remember how Newman complained about the likely results of the proclamation of the dogma of infallibility at Vatican I?

Br. Romuald: He predicted that there would be a dangerous veneration and adulation of the person and opinions of the reigning pope, contrary to the limited doctrine of infallibility defined at that council.

Br. Barsanuphius: Perhaps what we are experiencing today is, at long last, the sifting through and clarifying of the very problems Newman diagnosed. For there has been over a century of papal maximalism and positivism that sits uneasily with most of Catholic tradition, and we can see it pretty much self-destructing at this time.

Br. Romuald: In other words, we have had unreasonable expectations about the papacy, and now the Lord is putting us to the ultimate test, to see whether we are mature enough in our faith to deal with it.

Br. Barsanuphius: To put it more positively: this pontificate will force theologians to make more distinctions about the exercise of the papal office and the exact parameters of the obedience of the faithful than they have ever been required to make before. It used to be considered a rule of thumb—in your neoscholastic manuals, for instance—that the mere appearance of something in the *Acta Apostolicae Sedis* would justify making a religious submission of will and intellect to it. This latest publication rather abruptly puts an end to *that* exaggerated deference!

Br. Romuald: You mean, shows us that the assumptions of the 1950's are untenable?

Br. Barsanuphius: Right. The 1950's left us two striking examples to think about: the Assumption with a capital "a," and the assumptions of the liturgical reformers that gave us the "reformed Holy Week." The former is a dogma of the faith; the latter was a tragic rupture.

Br. Romuald: I know what you mean. For a long time I had this uncomfortable feeling that the Pacellian rites were a pastiche of old and modern bits, based on someone's clever idea of how things ought to go. It never seemed right.

Br. Barsanuphius: And when the monastery returned to the ancient rites of Holy Week, you know, the pre-Pacellian ones, I was—I have to say—just carried away by the awesomeness, the majesty, the overpowering *reality* of them. I felt almost crushed by their weight, and yet, oddly, free to be serious about the most serious thing of all.

Br. Romuald (after a silence): You are turning into a mystic on me, brother…

Br. Barsanuphius (smiling): You can blame that on the old liturgy!

Br. Romuald: The point is, we need a better rule than that neoscholastic automatism, which practically assumes that every incumbent of the papal throne will be a saint and a doctor of the Church to boot. We need something more in accord with the intentions and texts of Vatican I, not to mention the nuanced understanding, developed over nineteen centuries, of the inherent authority of Scripture, Tradition, and the Magisterium.

Br. Barsanuphius: What you say reminds me that in this regard, as in so many others, we are inferior to our forefathers, who, in addition to their other good qualities, tended to be more flexible, more realistic, more zealous, and more commonsensical than we are… Ah, do you hear the Vespers bell ringing? Let's go, so we're not late for *statio*.

Br. Romuald: Pray for me, brother. I never thought I'd live to see such times.

Br. Barsanuphius: Nor does any of us. But this is the age God willed for us—for you and me. And, as strange as it may seem, He chose *us* for these times, He wanted us to be *here*, living, praying, suffering. (*A few moments pass.*) You know how we've mentioned Newman a lot? There's a marvelous meditation of his, which has brought me much consolation over the years. My parents had me memorize it when I was a child, and it's never left me.

> God has created me to do Him some definite service;
> He has committed some work to me
> which He has not committed to another…
> Therefore I will trust Him.
> Whatever, wherever I am, I can never be thrown away.
> If I am in sickness, my sickness may serve Him;
> in perplexity, my perplexity may serve Him;
> if I am in sorrow, my sorrow may serve Him.
> My sickness, or perplexity, or sorrow
> may be necessary causes of some great end,
> which is quite beyond us.
> He does nothing in vain;
> He may prolong my life, He may shorten it;
> He knows what He is about.
> He may take away my friends,
> He may throw me among strangers,
> He may make me feel desolate,
> make my spirits sink,
> hide the future from me—
> still He knows what He is about.[12]

It is our job to offer up a pure sacrifice of praise, and to keep jealously the truth that He has imparted to us. This will be how we "save the Church." It will not happen any other way.

---

12. *Meditations and Devotions*, part III: Meditations on Christian Doctrine, §1, n. 2.

Br. Romuald: You have some wisdom beyond your years, young man. Let's be off.

9

Gnosticism, Liturgical Change, and Catholic Life

A Conversation in Vienna on April 2, 2017

Mr Wolfram Schrems: First of all, I would like to ask Professor Stark a question on a difficult but important topic. Professor Stark gave a brilliant talk in this very room two and a half years ago, namely on Tuesday, November 4th, 2014, in the presence of His Eminence Raymond Cardinal Burke, concerning the theological and philosophical foundations of the heresies of Walter Kasper, and on how a prevalent strand in moral theology today, namely Schelling's and Hegel's gnosticism, also applies, in a sense, to liturgy. Is the modern Mass a product of a legitimate evolution, or not? From the talks we have heard today, we must conclude that it is not a legitimate evolution; it is not a legitimate development. There are other more sinister ideologies underlying the new Mass. Since Professor Stark is an expert on this topic, his talk was published and enriched many, many people; it was translated into several languages. I would like to ask him to give us a brief introduction to the idea of gnosticism and the way in which it applies to the modern liturgical and theological discussion.

Dr Thomas Stark: Thank you. I want to use a simple approach. First of all, we have to see that the development of liturgy takes place in the context of theology. So, what we have in the background are certain ways in which Catholic teaching changed—not Catholic teaching understood as the Magisterium, but Catholic teaching that is brought to the public in the universities. And I want to start with something that happened just a few weeks ago.

A few weeks ago, the new superior general of the Jesuit order was asked about Our Lord's words on matrimony and on the dissolubility of marriage. And what he said was very interesting. First of all, he said: "Well, you know, Jesus used a certain language, he lived in the context of a certain culture, he had a certain public that he tried to reach with his words, but all these things have changed, and always change. Language changes, the cultural context changes, the people are changing... So, we have to reinterpret the words of Our Lord in these different contexts that are changing over the years and over the centuries." And then he said: "By the way, we didn't have tape recorders really to know what Christ actually said. What we have in the Scriptures is the interpretation of the authors of the Scriptures, how *they* understood the words of Our Lord. That means we don't have any real ground on which we can stand in our theological interpretation and our theological thought. Things always change. We don't really know what Our Lord said. It all depends on several changing contexts."

But this is only the first layer of the problem. This is the layer of, I will say, modern mentality. This modern mentality is illustrated by the song of Bob Dylan entitled "The Times They Are a-Changin'." This is what modern man thinks about culture, about even his own religion. But this is only the surface layer; there is a layer beneath that—the layer of ideology. This ideological layer is the layer of evolutionism. Evolution takes place—this is how modern man thinks —both in nature and in culture. Evolution means that we have developed from simple to complicated, from primitive to sophisticated. History, in nature as well as in society, is an upward-tending development which makes things better and better. For years now there have been very interesting discussions in America, where important scientists are questioning biological evolution with very good arguments. So we can see that not even in the biological sphere is this ideology of evolution really sufficient; or at least it looks as if things are changing in natural science.

But, underneath the layer of mentality and the layer of ideology, there is one even deeper layer, the layer of metaphysics. And the layer of metaphysics on which all these other things are grounded— the evolutionary ideology and the mentality that springs from it—is a metaphysics of gnosticism, which says in its core that not only is the world developing on an upward-tending course, but that the Absolute, which is the foundation of all reality, in itself develops. And the way it develops is that it flows into its own creation; the Divine-Absolute develops in its evolution, which takes place in nature and in culture. This gnostic metaphysics was already around when the Catholic Church began to lay down its theological foundations by means of Greek philosophy, around the second century. As theological thought in the Catholic Church developed, at the same time this alternative to Christianity that is Gnosticism also developed. And when you look into the history of thought you can see that each and every heretical movement in Church history, from ancient times through the Middles Ages until today, has always been based on this gnostic metaphysics.

The Church managed to minimize the influence of this gnostic metaphysics until the end of the Middle Ages, and from the fifteenth century on the whole thing exploded and began to poison our whole culture. European history from the fifteenth century until nowadays is a constant rise of gnosticism and of gnostic ideas, which were given sophisticated formulation by Hegel, who developed the most elaborate system of gnostic thought. And the problem is that in the nineteenth century—where the Catholic Church came under pressure from the liberal world, which led to all these struggles connected to the name of Pius IX and the *Syllabus of Errors* and all of the following popes who fought against modernism, which is liberalism within the Church—some Catholic intellectuals thought that the way to address some of these problems might be to adapt Catholic thought and Catholic teaching to some "new" metaphysical ideas that were invented at the beginning of the nineteenth century, connected especially to German idealism and especially to Schelling and Hegel. They tried to base Catholic teaching on the metaphysical ground of this German idealism and built a school, the so-called Tübingen school, which was very influential in the theological sphere in Germany and to which people like Kasper belonged (something they are very proud of).

And I think this evolutionary thought, grounded in gnosticism as its end, provides the context for the development of a theology in which the interpretation of the liturgy and the practice of it developed in the way that we have seen in the last decades.

Schrems: So, the underlying idea is the same as Darwin's, isn't it? If a fish changes enough, it becomes a man. And if an engineer develops an elaborate vacuum cleaner, then, after many missing links, a razor will emerge, or a laundry machine, or whatever!

I would like to ask our esteemed guest Professor Kwasniewski, is there a legitimate development within liturgy?

Dr Peter Kwasniewski: I was thinking, Professor Stark, as you were speaking, about a very important distinction that St Vincent of Lérins makes. Vincent was an early Church Father who wrote a work called the *Commonitorium*, which was essentially a lengthy warning against heresies arising from people who departed from tradition. That's his fundamental thesis: whenever you depart from tradition, from what's been handed down, then you will end up in heresy. And he makes the distinction between growth and change. An organism grows when it adds to itself without changing itself. So, as we grow up from children to adults, we remain the same person, we have the same name, the same dignity, the same DNA; all sorts of fundamental things about us remain the same, even though we develop in many accidental ways, often important but accidental ways. And he contrasts growth with *mutatio*. *Mutatio*, for him, is when one thing mutates into another and becomes a different essence. And he says for the Catholic religion to do that, that's what heresy is—a mutation rather than a growth.

So I think in the realm of the liturgy, there's absolutely no question that liturgy develops, not only in the Western sphere, with all the diverse rites—the Mozarabic Rite, the Ambrosian Rite, the Roman Rite, the Gallican Rite, the mixture of Gallican and Roman, and so on—but also in the Eastern sphere. I mean, as fixed as the Eastern liturgies are, the liturgy of Saint John Chrysostom still took centuries to develop, the liturgy of Saint Basil developed, and so on and so forth. And yet, these [developments] are additions being made to something that already exists, to a pre-existing kernel, and the kernel is devoutly respected, is revered, is jealously guarded, handed on with great love from one generation to the next. And because of the love and devotion of the people, they want to add *more* to the liturgy, to add (so to speak) bells and whistles, to add more incense or more processions or more preparatory prayers or more subsequent prayers or certain repetitions. So there's a kind of augmentation and elaboration of the liturgy. But you never have, in the East or the West, people coming to the liturgy and saying, "Okay, look, there's something wrong with this liturgy. We need to take it apart, divide it among thirty different *coetus* or committees,[1] and we'll assign the lectionary to this *coetus,* and the preparatory part [of Mass] to this *coetus,* and the Eucharistic Canon to this *coetus,* and we'll work for a few years very busily and glue it all together in the end, and say this is our new rite." That's *never* happened; it's inconceivable for Christians to do such a thing. And so in that sense, it seems clear that it's not a growth, but a *mutatio.*

Schrems: I would like to give the next turn to you [P. Edmund Waldstein], because you are the only one on the panel who lives a religious life with a very strict structure in a monastery. So, would you like to respond to Professor Kwasniewski? But I would also like to ask you: What is it like to experience the same liturgy every day? Is it boring? Is it dull? Should it be changed up? So maybe you could give us an inside glimpse of liturgy and of its development.

Pater Edmund Waldstein: Well, I would begin with what seems like a counterexample to what Dr Kwasniewski said, namely, with the liturgical reforms that were done within my own order, the Cistercian Order, at the time of its founding.

The Cistercians were founded with the ambition of returning to the original observance of the *Rule* of Saint Benedict. So they

---

1. Reference is made here to the many study groups (*coetus*)—45, in fact—of the *Consilium ad exsequendam Constitutionem de Sacra Liturgia,* the body, under the secretaryship of Annibale Bugnini, established by Paul VI to implement the Second Vatican Council's provisions for liturgical reform. Its work began in 1964 and would culminate in the preparation of new liturgical books for nearly every rite and ritual of the Catholic Church, most notably the Novus Ordo Missae of 1969.

wanted to remove the additions to the monastic rule that had been made by the monks of Cluny, already going back even to Benedict of Aniane. The monks of Cluny had added many prayers to the monastic liturgy, so that at Cluny, the liturgical prayer was almost perpetual. The monks would go into the cloister for five minutes for a break, then they would go back in the choir and keep singing. Everything was absorbed in the liturgy. When they did the baking of the hosts for Mass, for example, the grinding of the wheat was done vested in albs, and they sang the penitential psalms, then they mixed the wheat with other things, then put them in the oven. Everything was a liturgy. And the Cistercians said this is not what the *Rule* of Saint Benedict says, and we returned to the primitive observance. They abolished many, many additions that had been made by Cluny and returned to the liturgical office as it had been laid down by Saint Benedict, which divides the life of the monk between liturgical prayer, *lectio divina*, and work. Cluny monks didn't do any work. They had serfs that worked and they just spent the whole day praying. Sounds like heaven on earth, but the Cistercians said no. They were very austere. They allowed only a very little bit of gold; for example, the chalice for Mass was to be silver, and only the inside that touched the Precious Blood was allowed to be gold. And the ornamentation of the Churches was austere as well. You had only a crucifix and an image of Our Lady, and otherwise no statues or pictures in the Church. And the candlesticks were to be made of bronze, not gold or silver. So you have there what seems like a counterexample, where they want to return to the original *Gestalt*, the original form of the monastic liturgy, precisely by taking off additions. Maybe you could comment on that, before I then answer the question about my experience.

Kwasniewski: It's fascinating. In the history of the liturgy, you definitely have moments of expansion and moments of contraction. It seems to me, though, that the example that you're speaking of... if I could use a metaphor, it's a little bit like saying we don't want to have a seven-course meal, we want to have a three-course meal. So let's cut away some of the courses that are there. We don't attack the menu; we don't change the cuisine; we just say: we only want three courses. But there's a different kind of change that would be like going from a cooked meal to fast food, or going from Austrian food to Chinese food, or something like that. And that's something that you never see. It would be very strange if Roman Catholics decided one day: "Let's do Byzantine prayers, let's start to celebrate the liturgy of Saint John Chrysostom!" Beautiful liturgy—but it's not our rite, you know. So I think that that's the more radical kind of change. What you're talking about is, within the sphere of the liturgical offices already developed, choosing which ones fit best within your monastic life.

Schrems: What is your experience, do you feel a need for change? Or is it okay the way it goes?

Waldstein: I don't feel a need for change. Obviously, I feel a need for change in that I forever need to be more conformed to the liturgy that we say. We do not sing the Office as it was laid down in the *Holy Rule*. Saint Benedict says, after he gives the order of the Divine Office—which psalms are to be said at which hours—he then says that the monastery can change this order as long as they still pray all of the psalms that need to be sung in the week.

After the Council, there were many changes. In Heiligenkreuz, which of course is not most monasteries, we too made changes, and one of those changes is that we went from the traditional monastic one-week psalter to a two-week psalter. But even with a two-week psalter, I think the kind of effect that this repetition of the divine praises has is still there. Certainly, it would be better in many ways if we had not changed to the two-week psalter. But even so, we have the same words every two weeks; in fact, many of the psalms are repeated every day—for example, at Compline, every day the same three psalms. There is no spontaneity. There is no reacting to the situation in the moment. Every day at Compline we sing the same three psalms.

The monastic fathers compare the monks to farm animals in their stalls, ruminating, chewing their food over and over again, their fodder. The monks are chewing on the word of God over and over again and there's an inexhaustible wealth there. Saint Benedict says the monks should so sing that their hearts conform to their voices, their spirits conform to their voices: *ut mens nostra concordet voci nostrae.*[2] And that is a process that should take a whole lifetime. There's always a greater wealth there than you can exhaust in your lifetime. Before the reform in Heiligenkreuz, as in almost all monasteries, the custom was to pray Compline in darkness, because everyone knew it by heart.

Kwasniewski: I heard an Armenian priest recently talking about his experience of the liturgy. Their divine liturgy is very stable and very uniform. They have few things that change. And he said that a woman in Germany once approached him and said: "Father, don't you get tired of praying the same liturgy over and over again?" And he said to her: "Would you get tired of seeing your mother every day, or seeing your husband every day?" And if the answer is yes, then there's something wrong.

So, getting back to the point about gnosticism, that metaphysics of flux: it's Heraclitian in a way, Heraclitian flux. The Catholic understanding of reality, it seems to me, is much more fundamentally rooted in the concept of immutability, of unchangeableness, than in the concept of change. Obviously, change is real. But God is unchanging. He is immutable. And human nature is also unchanging. What man is is always the same, from Adam to the last man who will ever live on this earth. And therefore, all things being equal, the liturgy ought to be more unchanging than changing, in order to correspond to who God is and who man is.

Stark: It's interesting that you mention Heraclitus, because in my opinion, the choice between Heraclitus and Parmenides is the big struggle in Greek philosophy. And they both got it wrong. Heraclitus anticipates Hegel, and Parmenides anticipates Spinoza *in nuce*. These are similar constructions. And the one who finally got it right was Plato, because he distinguished between cosmos and the divine Absolute which created the cosmos, and thereby invented the possi-

2. *Holy Rule*, chapter 19.

bility of thinking of change within stability and stability within change.

The problem with the concept of tradition and identity in many theologians—and I have gotten deeper and deeper in that by studying the works of Kasper, which I have studied for two years—is that they have a concept of identity and a concept of tradition very much influenced by this concept represented by Heraclitus. In Heraclitus's philosophy, nothing has an identity, with one exception: the structures in which the flux continues, which is led by the *logos*. And this is why Heraclitus as well as Parmenides are heathens: they think that there is nothing else outside of the cosmos, but that the divine and the cosmos are identical, which is the basis of paganism, in the way I use the term. For the one conception, in Parmenides, it is just "the One" in a numerical sense, and for the other conception, in Heraclitus, which is more sophisticated, the only thing that's really stable is the *logos*. Everything else changes, but the *logos* in itself *needs* these changes to exist.

And now we have a situation, under the rise of gnosticism, in which very many people are not aware that they are influenced by it. But this influence of gnosticism leads to a concept of tradition, of identity, which I think I can find in Walter Kasper: we have a condition where nothing in tradition stays stable. "Tradition" is purely development, a process of connection with something earlier; this is what tradition is all about. Within this development, everything can change. There's nothing identical—and that matches very well with postmodern thought. For example, postmodernists, making reference to Freud and other psychologists and sociologists, deny that there is something like a personal identity. So we live in a postmodern age where we believe that identity is something that just doesn't exist. And the problem is that we have this old heresy of gnosticism which has influenced our theology, and our theology suits very well the postmodern mentality, all of which makes this whole mixture so explosive and so dangerous.

Waldstein: I would just like to say one more thing about the difference between reform and revolution, looking at monastic history. There's a very amusing passage in a history of the Cistercian order written by an American author from the abbey of Dallas. It's a chapter on the second order of the Cistercians, that is, the sisters. And he says that if you look at the history of the Cistercian nuns, from Saint Bernard of Clairvaux to the present day, you see periodically their reforms. And their reforms always have one main point: the main point is always to restore the strictness of the enclosure, always, throughout the whole history of the order. You see this very clearly in Marie Angélique [Arnauld] of Port-Royal: she slams the door in the face of her parents, reestablishing the enclosure... Except that in the reforms after Vatican II, the reform is to *open up* the enclosure!

Schrems: This is a good occasion to pass on to another topic of our discussion. Professor Kwasniewski is a great fan of Msgr Robert Hugh Benson and his work, which I also very much appreciate. One of these works, a historical novel set in the time of the English Reformation, is called *By What Authority?* This question is not answered in the book, but the title is excellent: by what authority did King Henry VIII change the religion of England? By what authority did Cranmer and Cromwell and all these fellows persecute the Church?

So my question to Professor Kwasniewski is: By what authority did Paul VI introduce a new missal? I'm well aware that none of us is a canon lawyer, but despite this, we must ask ourselves: Who gave the authority to make such a big transition? Was the missal of Paul VI promulgated in the juridically correct way? The question is urgent because Benedict XVI said in *Summorum Pontificum* that the old rite has never been abrogated. But every person living in the 1970's experienced that it *had* been abrogated, abolished, suppressed. So what is your position on this topic?

Kwasniewski: It's a very difficult set of questions that you've asked, and there are actually several questions there.

The first, most basic point I would make is that the understanding of the office of the pope seems to have changed under certain modern pressures. I'm not sure exactly how to put my finger on it, but Cardinal Newman talks about the office of the papacy as a *remora*, a barrier, against change. Newman, when he does his historical overview of the function of the papacy, says that in almost every case in Church history, the pope is the one who says: "No, we will not change. This new idea, this new practice, we don't know it, we've never seen it here, we're suspicious of it, we reject it." And in fact, the Roman liturgy was one of the simplest liturgies of all the liturgies, Eastern and Western, because although everywhere the liturgies developed and grew in various ways, in Rome the conservative spirit was so strong that its liturgy grew much more slowly. So, if you have a pope who's driving innovation or novelty, there's something wrong with that picture; that's an overstepping of the office of the papacy, an exaggeration of it, and something that the Eastern Orthodox can and should object to. They have a right to object to that; that's an office that is too big for itself.

When you get to the specifically liturgical question, here I have to agree with Msgr Klaus Gamber that the rite Pope Paul VI promulgated in 1969 cannot be called the Roman rite. Gamber calls it the "modern rite," or the "modern papal rite."[3] And he says that from the point of view of a liturgical scholar, the scholar of liturgical history, it's impossible to see this as the Roman rite. It can be seen as loosely *based on* the Roman rite, but it's far more different from the preceding Roman rite than the Roman rite was from many other uses and rites that existed in the West. There's a much bigger gap there.

So the question then becomes, I think, can a pope promulgate a *new* liturgical rite, even if it's not the Roman rite? Can he invent a rite and say: This is valid? It seems to me that you can't simply deny that he has the power to institute such a rite, but you can deny that he has the moral authority to do so. *Ought* he to do so? Not: *can* he do so, but *should* he do so? And there, my personal opinion is no, he does not have the moral authority to do that, and it's a kind of abuse of papal power to do so. And therefore I'm not surprised at how many evil consequences have come from it, because I think that you can judge a tree by its fruits.

---

3. See Klaus Gamber, *The Reform of the Roman Liturgy: Its Problems and Background*, trans. Klaus D. Grimm (Fort Collins, CO: Roman Catholic Books, n.d.), 27–39, 91–95.

Stark: It was Martin Mosebach who said imposing a new liturgy on the Church was an act of tyranny, in the sense that tyranny in ancient times consisted of changing ancient rules or laws.[4]

Schrems: So it was imposed on the Church without the Church really desiring a new rite. Then is the promulgation of the new missal deficient, juridically speaking?

Kwasniewski: This much is clear. When you look into the details, the promulgation of the new missal was done in a confused or clumsy way. I've read several canonical studies of it, and the language of Paul VI is not as clear as Pope Pius V's language was when it came to the Tridentine Missal of 1570 with *Quo Primum*. There, the language is very carefully crafted; it was exceptionally clear. In the original text of the Constitution *Missale Romanum* of 1969, it was not clear at all whether the legislator intended an abrogation or an obrogation or a derogation. It was unclear. And then, when the official version was published in the *Acta Apostolicae Sedis*, sentences were added to it that were not in the original version, because they were trying to clarify its effect. And even those clarifying sentences were unclear.

Stark: Who did that? The Consilium?

Kwasniewski: I don't know. But the text of *Missale Romanum* was published first and then later appeared in *Acta Apostolicae Sedis* with a new paragraph at the end because people had asked questions. And even the new paragraph was not very clear. So I think when you look into it canonically you can see why Pope Benedict was able to say that the old rite, the *usus antiquior*, had never been abrogated, because it hadn't.

But it gets even more complicated. I heard a canon lawyer explain that there's a distinction between the legitimacy of a liturgical book itself and then the right of a priest to use that book. These are obviously intimately connected, but they're not exactly the same. So you can have a legitimate liturgical book but also have a priest who

---

4. Cf. Mosebach, *Heresy of Formlessness*, 9.

doesn't have the permission to use that book. And if you make this distinction, I think it can be said that the missal of Pope Pius V, as emended by various popes up until 1962, was never abrogated, but Pope Paul VI intended to take away permission from the priests to *use* that missal. He would have the authority to say: "No, you can't use that book; you have to use this other book." Again, he may have had the authority, but the question again is, should he have done so? And that's why in *Summorum Pontificum*, Pope Benedict says not only that the old missal is not abrogated, but also that each priest has permission to use this book without any permission from anybody else. He had to say both of those things.

Waldstein: I don't want to give any answer to that question,[5] maybe because of a defect in me; I don't want to give a wrong answer. I celebrate both forms of the Roman rite, more often the new form and about once a week the old form. Growing up as a child and as a youth and so on, I went usually to the new form. I think whatever ends up being the position you take on whether it's legitimate or properly promulgated—this form of the Roman rite—we know that God uses everything for the good of the elect. Even things that were begun in confusion and trespass of power can be used for the good. And that's certainly been my experience. So, even from the liturgy celebrated with the new missal, I've gained much spiritual fruit, and I hope that I've been able to share that spiritual fruit with others. Thus I think that it's possible to say both—both that this was an abuse of papal power, but also that God has been able to use it for good.

Kwasniewski: It does seem, though, that it would be important ultimately for a rectification to take place. That is to say, I think what Benedict XVI envisioned, although how it would happen is much more difficult to say, is a final outcome where the opposition of the two forms or the abyss between the two forms would be closed somehow. And he never really explained how that would happen; he gave some very generic suggestions about mutual enrichment

---

5. That is: By what authority did Paul VI introduce a new missal?

and so on. But nevertheless, it is irregular for the Roman rite to have two forms. It's a strange phenomenon. It's never happened in the 2,000-year history of the Church; we've always had one Roman rite. We've had many other Western rites and Eastern rites, but there's always been one Roman rite—the rite of the papal curia, to be more exact—and now we have two forms of it. Objectively, it's an odd and strange situation, and it does need a healing, even though I grant what you're saying.

Schrems: I would like to ask Professor Kwasniewski about the solutions and the required habits of the lay people. Because, as we see, many lay Catholics are interested in liturgical questions and feel very uneasy about the developments that have occurred in the last 50 years. Professor Kwasniewski wrote a very interesting paper called "A Defense of Liturgy as Carolingian Court Ritual."[6] I found this very interesting and also hilarious in a way, because you say: "Very well, this *is* a Carolingian court ritual—but so what? What's the problem with it? That's how it should be." Maybe you could develop some points on how lay people should react to the liturgical catastrophe. Should we boycott the Novus Ordo altogether? Should we go, as I do, to the Ukrainian Greek Catholics or to the Armenians, if we don't get any access to the old [Roman] rite? So, what are our objectives? How do you deal with the situation?

Kwasniewski: It's hard. It's a very hard situation because some people have an easier time than others finding a reverent liturgy that spiritually nourishes them so that they can give glory and honor to God. I have many friends who are fortunate enough to live where the Fraternity of Saint Peter or the Institute of Christ the King has a chapel and an apostolate and they go regularly, sometimes even daily. I think that's ideal. If a Catholic can attend the old liturgy, then I think he ought to do so as a rule. Otherwise, he's depriving himself of so much of his heritage, his tradition, of the spiritual riches that are there. For me, if I can go to an *usus antiquior*, then I do and it's not even a question. If I can't find one, then the second

6. Published at *New Liturgical Movement* on January 30, 2017.

question would be: is there an Eastern rite liturgy available? Because the Eastern liturgies have not been corrupted; they have not suffered the damage, and they are also equally rich depositories of the Catholic faith. Although that's not ideal, because it's not your own rite; you should worship in your own rite. Many people find themselves in the situation where they don't have either of these options available, unless you drive for a really long time. And so you have to go to the most reverent Mass you can find to fulfill your Mass obligation.

And apart from that, don't forget that the liturgy is not only the Mass; the liturgy is also the Divine Office—the breviary, the Liturgy of the Hours—and I encourage people to get to know Compline, get to know Vespers, especially in their traditional Roman forms. These can be very nourishing, prayed either as an individual or with your family. My family and I pray Vespers together from the *Monastic Diurnal*;[7] we love to do Vespers. Every day we come home and pray Vespers before dinner, even when there's no Mass available. I think those are some of the options.

I will say this much. I'm very impressed with my fellow American Catholics. I know people who will drive an hour or more to get to Mass on Sunday in the old form, because it's so important for their family's spirituality to be connected in that way to the liturgy.

Schrems: There's the question of how to bring the second generation into heaven, too! As you are a father of a family, how can lay people nowadays act so that their children don't get lost?

Kwasniewski: What I've seen with my children and with children in other families is that they quickly see the difference between a liturgy that is focused on God—giving glory to Him, thanking Him, praising Him, saying sorry to Him when one has sinned, adoring His presence and so on—and a liturgy that is community-centered

---

7. A book that contains, in Latin and English, the daytime hours of the Benedictine office, originally published by St John's Abbey in Collegeville and now reprinted by St Michael's Abbey in Farnborough. There are several editions from the 1940s through the early 1960s.

or is distracting, has lots of different activities going on, all of those many problems we don't need to rehearse here. Children quickly see the difference between these two things. And I think it's confusing and harmful to them to go back and forth between these two worlds. You need to pick the way that is going to inculcate the right spirit, the right virtues, the right mentality, the right dispositions. And those things are sadly lacking in many communities.

Schrems: You are also an expert on Gregorian chant, you teach Gregorian chant to students at Wyoming Catholic College. Maybe you could give us a brief sketch of what Gregorian chant is all about and how it relates to liturgy.

Kwasniewski: I wouldn't call myself an expert. I know some experts. But I do love Gregorian chant. I sing it and I teach it.

I think Gregorian chant is more important than people realize because it's not just a decoration of the liturgy, like the ornaments on a Christmas tree. Gregorian chant grew up with the Roman liturgy and developed at the same time. It's like the flesh over the bones of the liturgy, or like the clothing of the Roman rite—however you want to think of it. It's intimately a part of this rite. It is the Roman rite in music; that's what chant is. So when you sing the Kyrie, the Gloria, the Sanctus, the Agnus Dei, when you sing the Introit, the Gradual, the Tract, the Offertory, the Communion, you're singing the liturgy. These are not just motets or hymns or whatever; this is the liturgy itself. So I would make the claim—maybe this would seem too audacious for you—I would make the claim that Gregorian chant is as much a part of the Roman liturgy as the Roman Canon itself is. How do you know if you have the Roman rite? When you have the Roman Canon. If you don't have the Roman Canon, you don't have the Roman rite, you have something else. If you're going to *sing* the Roman rite—as you should, because the Mass ought to be sung—then you need to have the *music* of the Roman rite, which is Gregorian chant, as Vatican II said.[8] It's bone of its bone, flesh of its flesh; it's so intimately connected.

8. *Sacrosanctum Concilium*, n. 116.

Sometimes you see traditional communities that use the *usus antiquior* and love it but they have lots of vernacular music or lots of organ music and the chant is not really present, or not present very much. This is a problem in a traditional community, because they're not realizing that by acting in this way they've got a kind of Protestant mix-and-match. They don't have the authentic liturgy.

Stark: You make an interesting point. Personally, I love, for example, the Masses written by Mozart or by Schubert. I love this music and I sang this music in a parish choir for many years. But I also lived with the Eastern rite for several years. I lived in a place where the *usus antiquior* was not available to me and I went to the Eastern rite and got used to this approach that they have to liturgy. And after that, I finally understood why Pius X said somewhere, or wrote, that operatic music doesn't have a place in the liturgy.[9] And I thought: "That's exactly right." No Byzantine or Eastern rites, no Christian who is accustomed to the Eastern rite, could understand that we use the music of Mozart for liturgy, because they and we have a music that is *just* liturgical music and we should stick with that. We should hear the Mozart Masses in a concert hall, but we should use the Gregorian chant for liturgy. I'm convinced of that. And what do you think about early polyphony?

Kwasniewski: This is great. I thought it would be heresy for me to say anything [negative] about Mozart and Schubert in Vienna! I love their music too, absolutely love it. I've sung Mozart Masses. I've sung Schubert Masses. Joseph Ratzinger, in his book *Spirit of the Liturgy*, talks about three moments of crisis in the history of Church music. The first moment of crisis was around the time of the Council of Trent. The second crisis was in 1903, around the time of Pius X's *Tra le Sollecitudini*. And the third crisis is today, during and after the Council. And he says what each of these crisis moments has in common is the irruption of the secular into the sacred, into the temple. So at the Council of Trent, you had various secular songs or themes coming into the Church music, and a lot of vernacular...

---

9. In the motu proprio *Tra le Sollecitudini* (November 3, 1903), nn. 5–6.

Stark: Because it was so popular for the Protestants and it was successful.

Kwasniewski: Exactly. Then, with Pius X, it was the influence of opera on sacred music [that was the problem]. And with our situation today, it's the influence of pop music or folk music or pseudo-folk music on the liturgy. But in all three cases, you have sacred music being redesigned, recast, in the form of secular music, so that when someone hears it, they're tapping their toes, they're thinking "oh, this is great, I'm being entertained!," and they've stopped worshipping God. That's the problem with secular music coming into the liturgy. For this reason Pius X enunciated a rule—a very perfect rule—saying that the more music is like Gregorian chant, the more suited it is for the temple of God, and the less like it, the less suited. And then he said that sacred music should not, even in its external features, remind us of secular music and secular things. The worst case example of this would be to bring in an electric guitar and drums, which are associated only with secular music; that's the desacralization of liturgy.

Now obviously, Mozart and Schubert are great composers; their music is beautiful. They don't have the problem of pop music and suchlike. But the problem with their music is that it's strongly metrical, it's operatic in style, it's complex in style, and it's very entertaining. And so it tends to detract from the meditation, the purification, the focus and the adoration that we need to give to God. I know that when *I* hear a Mozart Mass, I'm just entertained by it; maybe other people have a different experience. But sacred polyphony of the Middle Ages and the Renaissance is much closer to the spirit and even the musical language of the chant, and therefore harmonizes with "the spirit of the liturgy," as Guardini and Ratzinger would say.

Schrems: As we're drawing to a close now, I would like to thank the gentlemen around the table—Professor Kwasniewski, Reverend Father Edmund, Professor Stark—for their participation. I think it was a great discussion. Thank you all for the insights you have given us.

10

May We Question
the Liturgical Reform?

William: My good fellow, I simply can't go along with your position that the Novus Ordo is inherently defective. A pope could never promulgate a liturgy that was harmful to the faithful.

Terence: Bill, you amaze me! What prevents you from seeing what seems an obvious fact to me and so many other Catholics? *Of course* a pope can do that, because Paul VI did it *in spades*, and here we are, wallowing in the mess. The mess is all around us, in the countless boring and banal—if not irreverent and sacrilegious—liturgies celebrated every day.

William: That's only because of the way people have chosen to celebrate it, Terry. There's nothing wrong with the liturgy in itself—nor could there be. Blame the driver, don't blame the car!

Terence: Let's try to step back. Your hesitations proceed, if I'm not mistaken, from an underlying anxiety about what the fallout would be, if one admitted that it *had* been a mistake for Paul VI to promulgate a new Order of Mass (and a new order of everything he could get his hands on). What would happen to the life or duties of Catholics if one believed that the new liturgy was a deviation, a dead end; that the traditional liturgy preceding it was fundamentally sound and already capable of meeting the needs of "modern man"; and that one ought to embrace it again, as much as one could?

William: Yes, quite so. Now that you say it, I believe that the fallout would be considerable. I don't think we could trust the pope about anything, if we can't trust him about the liturgy. It might undermine the whole system of Catholic belief and practice.

Terence: It may surprise you to hear that I can't see any significant fallout for me. Critical as I am about the liturgical reform, I still profess the Creed and accept all the defined dogmas and morals clearly taught by the Church. I strive to pattern my life after the lives of Our Lord, His Mother, and the long line of saints. I receive and pass on the teaching contained in the authoritative catechisms. I worship God in the liturgy and sacraments of apostolic tradition that the Church has handed down as the primary source of her sanctity. Really, the only difference between me and a Catholic of a century ago is that he would have had easier access to these things, whereas I must seek them out with determination, in the teeth of the ignorance, error, hostility, and indifference of clergy and laity alike.

William: That's rather strongly put, but I suppose it makes you not very much different from a Catholic of the Reformation period who, living amidst ecclesiastical corruption and doctrinal confusion, worked hard to know his faith and live according to it.

Terence: Exactly. Does this mean that I am on a trajectory towards repudiating the office of the papacy or its ultimate authority to define or adjudicate matters of faith or morals? Far from it.

William: Then how do you make sense out of the enormous lapse in papal prudence demanded by your position? Wouldn't it undermine the reverence we owe the pope, and the confidence we place in him?

Terence: Here we get to the nub of the question. The papal office does not *in principle* exclude grievous flaws in the prudential order and in matters of non-definitive teaching. Such flaws may include the imprudent approval of a liturgical or sacramental rite defective in its secondary elements (that is, not in its form and matter), which are liable to occasion an inadequate or faulty understanding of the mysteries with which it deals. Scripture, Tradition, and Magisterium have never told us that this is impossible; it is not ruled out by the doctrine of papal infallibility as defined by Vatican I; therefore it is possible.

William: I would need to study Vatican I more carefully to assess your claim.

Terence: In addition to what the Magisterium itself says about its own conditions and limitations, we are also supposed to take seriously the evidence of our reason, our senses, our wits. God is the author of nature as much as He is the author of the supernatural. When we can see a disaster, we are to call it a disaster, and react accordingly. When a hurricane strikes, we don't wait for the government or the police to verify that a hurricane has occurred, as if we couldn't figure it out ourselves. Instead, we roll up our sleeves and start rescuing people, giving them food and water, cleaning up debris, and rebuilding. That's what traditionalists are doing in the Church. The monster tsunami hit, the damage was unbelievable, and the work of restoration has taken decades and will take decades more.

William: As usual, Terry, you speak extravagantly. I will stick with my usual line: if a layman or cleric comes away from the new liturgy with a misunderstanding about faith or morals, it is his own fault, since it was not *required* of him that he misunderstand anything—as would occur in the ambit of an explicitly heretical liturgy like that of the Calvinists.

Terence: That's not convincing, because the competent authority has a duty to provide such aids to understanding as human nature requires, and to avoid, as much as possible, anything that might readily suggest a false understanding. If vast numbers misunderstand what they have been given, there is a problem in the thing that was given, and the blame for this problem falls squarely on the one who gave it. One could make a similar argument about providing necessary aids to reverent celebration, such as fixed rituals with clear and adequate rubrics.

William: Be patient with me, as I'm still learning the ins and outs of this debate. Could you offer some examples?

Terence: The Novus Ordo *removes* traditional aids to understanding and worshiping rightly—this, after all, is what orthodoxy means: right doctrine and right worship, inseparably—and *includes* antiquarian or novel elements that suggest a false understanding of the Mass—for example, anachronistically returning to ancient Eucharistic practices that, coming *after* the development of medieval piety whose effects extended right into the modern world, had and could only have had a modernist inflection with the result of a weakening of faith in the Real Presence. Moreover, the dubious or explicitly modernist opinions of the new liturgy's compilers are well documented, which establishes that the very ones who put it together *intended* to remove certain aids and introduce certain novelties.

William: That's pretty damning, if it's true.

Terence: It's documented by the very people who revised the liturgy in the sixties and seventies.

William: You'll have to show me some of those sources later, when we're savoring Manhattans in your library. But let's assume you are right about what the reformers intended to do. How does this implicate the pope?

Terence: Can we get away with saying that a pope who patronizes such a product—a product of questionable theories, suspicious innovations, and manifest departures from the general consensus of the Council Fathers as formulated in *Sacrosanctum Concilium*—and then promulgates it for the Church of the Latin Rite is *not*, in a real sense, *responsible* for the deleterious effects that this new liturgy has had on the faithful? Can we say that he is not, in any way, answerable for its defects?

William: I don't see how we could.

Terence: Both natural reason and the judgment of faith would resoundingly answer No. This pope, Montini by name, is responsible for the evil of rupture; he is answerable for each and every one of the numberless abuses of the rite he promulgated, because in the manner of its redaction as well as in the manner of its very existence and operation, it departs from the sure path of tradition and opens the way to false inculturation, pluralism without end, and celebratory individualism, egoism, and narcissism.

William: I'm uncomfortable with where you're going, but it's hard for me to deny the plausibility of it. The pope is responsible for what he promulgates—and if its flaws are built in, so to speak, then he is as much their author as Bugnini or any other member of the Consilium. Or rather, he is even *more* their author, because he formally adopts the work as his own when he puts it forward authoritatively under his name.

Terence: You've got it.

William: But why are you so sure that the results of the reform have been uniformly bad?

Terence: I don't need to say all bad; just *mostly* bad. Can anyone seriously doubt that the new liturgy has had deleterious effects since its coercive introduction almost half a century ago? Quite apart from the statistics about devastating declines in Mass attendance throughout the Catholic world (a trend that began in the first fervor of liturgical experimentation in the 1960's and continues to this day, as the relentless closing of churches reminds us), there has been massive confusion about what the Mass *is*, and whether the Lord is truly present in the Eucharist, and how the priest at the altar differs from the layman, and other basics (basics!) of the Catholic Faith—even among those Catholics who still *attend* Mass and who are polled with simple questions that a first communion candidate in the 1950's could have answered with flying colors. Above all, one dare not ask Catholics whether the Mass is a sacrifice. Almost the only ones who will answer "yes" and could offer a simple explanation of their answer are Catholics who attend Mass with an Ecclesia Dei community, the SSPX, or one of the few dozen diocesan parishes worldwide that have a sound liturgical life.

William: Surely, many if not most of these problems take us back to wayward implementation, bad preaching, and the lack of good Catholic schools?

Terence: You are conveniently sidestepping the fact that the new Mass was everywhere perceived as inviting and even requiring a tradition-lite, improvisatory instantiation topped with storytelling preaching—and that nothing substantive was ever done to prevent this from happening, or to castigate it wherever it was habitual.

William: But there have been so many Vatican documents…

Terence: Oh, don't start on that! The endless stream of toothless documents, a mountain of inefficacious verbiage, is a sad testimony to the utter failure of genuine pastoral governance—ironic in an age that has adopted the word "pastoral" for its special descriptor. If there was a genuine desire to restore sacrality, reverence, beauty, solemnity, seriousness, good music, and so forth to the liturgy, it would all have come long ago. It has not and never will, because the Novus Ordo isn't *fundamentally, inflexibly, dogmatically* committed to the traditional vision of worship—and neither are the popes or bishops who support it.

William: So you think that the Novus Ordo is doomed to fail—that it cannot be turned right?

Terence: There's no reason to beat around the bush: the simple act of jettisoning the inherited liturgy, which was beloved across the ages and across the globe, and the imposition of a massively different neo-liturgy on a body of faithful that was not asking for it, more than adequately explains why its use was not blessed by God with the fruitfulness characteristic of the one true Church or the universal acceptance that could be expected for a papal act.

William: Say more what you mean.

Terence: Its bad fruits were immediately apparent, and its lack of acceptance by certain members of the laity and clergy was a poignant sign that something had gone seriously wrong—a sign that has not diminished but grown in the subsequent decades, down to the present. Except in those places that had a longstanding rite of their own and chose to hold on to it (as per the guidelines in *Quo Primum*), the Tridentine liturgy was accepted throughout the Catholic world with ever-increasing unanimity. In stark contrast, the new rite of Paul VI generated controversy from the start. It was called into question and resisted by a not-inconsiderable number of Catholics, both famous and obscure, in different parts of the world, and never won over everyone for whom it was intended. Each year that passes, more Catholics around the world effectively reject this botched reform as they return to the blessings of traditional worship. There has never been anything like it in Church history. That should tell us something about the limits of anyone's ability—be he the undisputed ruler of the known world, or the plenipotent pope of Rome—to dictate to reality how it must behave!

William: You are evidently not of the opinion of certain bloggers who think that traditionalism is a short-lived flash-in-the-pan, destined to go the way of Amish irrelevance...

Terence: Leaving aside the fascinating question of how irrelevant the Amish actually are when compared with the last gasps of mainline Protestantism, yes, I don't share those excessively optimistic views. Despite the vain wishes of its fabricators, the Novus Ordo Missae is *never* going to be able to establish itself as the only form of the Roman rite. Communities centered around the traditional Mass are yielding a disproportionately large harvest of priestly and religious vocations, arising from their consistently larger and better-catechized families.

William: You have to admit, though, that Pope Francis and his supporters around the world are doing their level best to stamp out the traditionalists.

Terence: When traditional Catholics are persecuted, as they have been during this pontificate, they do not give up or go away. If the blood of martyrs is the seed of Christianity, something analogous is true of the thrusting-aside of traditionalists, which only increases their intense work and prayer for the true reform of the Church, and confirms their assessment of the fundamentally modernist orientation of their enemies, which is not hard to prove in any case.

William: Don't you think there's a danger of traditionalists developing a martyr complex, and thinking themselves the "righteous remnant" because they are a badly treated minority?

Terence: Traditionalists are, in point of fact, generally regarded and treated as if we were worse than all other heretics or schismatics, and why? Because we believe and pass on what every Catholic used to believe for centuries. To me, this is a glowing sign that we're on the right path, the narrow path that leads to renewal. Renewal always comes from total commitment to Catholic truth in its integrity and plenitude. If we look at reform movements throughout history, we can see that they are always the work of a few, not of the many. The many are too comfortable in their positions of power or their assumptions about "the way things are." The few see things differently, envision something better. It is a privilege to suffer as a Catholic from the assaults of Catholics; it is a privilege to suffer for Jesus Christ and the Faith of our fathers instead of giving way to the ersatz faith peddled by the old boys' club.

William: We seem to have gone rather far afield from our original question. Do you mind if I come back to it?

Terence: Not at all.

William: Here is what I am committed to saying at all costs. The pope, when promulgating a liturgy, cannot promulgate a sacramentally invalid liturgy or one that contains positive error in faith or morals.

Terence: That's all your position boils down to? Then there's no disagreement between us.

William: You have to say more, Terry. Don't leave me hanging.

Terence: I don't know whether to call it a matter of faith or a conclusion deducible from a matter of faith, but I am convinced—and I believe that traditionalists in general would agree—that the pope *cannot* promulgate an invalid liturgy or one that contains positive error in faith or morals. Unpacked, this claim means that any papally promulgated sacramental rite will contain at least the form and matter required for the completion of that sacrament, and that one would not be able to establish that it expressly denies any article of faith or asserts claims that could *only* be construed as heretical.

William: So far, so good.

Terence: It does *not* follow, however, that the whole content of the Catholic Faith would have to be *found* in a papally promulgated rite. There is no reason it could not give a gravely inadequate expression to certain doctrines, or contain ambiguities susceptible to heretical interpretation. On the contrary, a valid rite could be defective in expressing the dogmatic and moral content of the Faith, and superficial or ambiguous enough to make heretical interpretation not only possible but probable. It could, in addition, allow or prompt a lack of due devotion, deficient reverence, and even sacrilege.

William: Once again, examples would help. What kind of defects are you referring to?

Terence: One example would be the deliberate omission throughout the Novus Ordo of 1 Corinthians 11:27–29, where unworthy Eucharistic communion is sternly warned against. This is no minor point of doctrine, given that both Scripture and the liturgy connect unworthy reception with the soul's eternal damnation!

William: I see your point, and concede it.

Terence: Some ultramontanists claim far more than you and I are claiming. For instance, they say that a papally promulgated liturgy is necessarily well-ordered; that it necessarily promotes the good of the Church as a whole; that it is incapable of having deleterious effects on the body of the faithful due to omissions, ambiguities, additions, or other modifications. I'm sorry to have to puncture their pretty balloons, but there is absolutely *no way* to prove such claims, quite apart from the difficulty of sustaining them in the face of mountains of contrary evidence. Claims of this nature are absurdly overstated and make a mockery of the Catholic doctrine of the papacy itself.

William: Let me summarize, to make sure I understand. The Catholic traditionalist does not assert that the Novus Ordo Missae embodies positive error in faith and morals. He does claim, however, that it is not in continuity with the tradition of the Roman Rite, and that this discontinuity has had catastrophic effects on the actual life of the Church. The practice of the faith has in fact declined *due* to what was done to the liturgy, and orthodox belief and morals have in fact suffered *due* to the omissions, ambiguities, modifications, and tolerated abuses of the new liturgy.

Terence: Will, you've summed it up perfectly.

William: All the same, Terry, I still feel you're being unfair to the Novus Ordo. You assume that it will be done in a flawed manner—which, admittedly, it often is. In argumentation, however, we should assume the Novus Ordo as Paul VI promulgated and intended it.

Terence: It is completely artificial to talk about some pristine Novus Ordo that measures all others, like the standard meter bar fashioned in the French Enlightenment. If you are hoping to find the new liturgy celebrated in full observance of the *General Instruction of the Roman Missal* and according to a Ratzingerian hermeneutic of continuity—that is, in Latin for the unchanging parts (as called for by Vatican II), with Gregorian chant (as called for by Vatican II), *ad orientem* (as the very rubrics of the Ordo Missae presuppose), without lay ministers of holy communion, and so forth—you might as well plan on making a pilgrimage to the Oratory in London, Oxford, or Toronto. You won't find this rare bird in your neighborhood aviary.

William: But surely what you've described is how it is *supposed* to be?

Terence: That, my friend, is where you are mistaken. If Paul VI had given the Church something *definite*, then we could have entertained your proposal. If he gave us something designedly malleable, subject to inculturation, adaptation, and variation, the almost countless abuses of which are tolerated everywhere, can we even talk about whether "the new liturgy" is a good thing or a bad thing? *What are we even talking about?* The very fact that it is so indefinite, indeterminate, and intractable is an unanswerable strike against it—a sign either that something is wrong with the form as such or that the hierarchy (including the popes) have been guilty of grave dereliction in their responsibility of watching over the liturgy and ensuring that the faithful have access to it in its integral fullness. Either way, the buck stops there, at the shoes, red or black, of the fisherman.

William: We are talking about what Paul VI himself had in mind and intended.

Terence: Unless you're a mind-reader of extraordinary facility, good luck with Montini's mind, which seems to have changed depending on the last person he spoke with. On one day he's telling people to retain Latin and chant, and a week later he's praising the virtues of vernacularity! A modern-day Abelard could write a new *Sic et Non* using Paul VI's writings.[1] Moreover, are we seriously going to say that it makes no difference what kind of modernist theology the compilers of the Novus Ordo had—as if, once Paul VI promulgated the new missal, all the erroneous assumptions behind it evaporated and the book was suddenly healed, in a kind of papal miracle? As if the removal of the Septuagesima season, contrary to ancient tradition and human psychology, doesn't matter at all, because once Paul VI promulgated the denuded calendar of 1969, it must be the *faithful's* fault if they don't get out of the streamlined new calendar everything their forefathers got out of the old one?

William: You are always putting so much emphasis on externals!

Terence: Do the aesthetics, the outward signs, of worship have no impact on subjective belief? Or are we going to say, again and again, that any failure on the part of the faithful to get what they should out of the Mass is exclusively their own fault—not the fault of a liturgy stripped of precisely those semiotic elements and ascetical practices that transmitted and reinforced moral and dogmatic truths?

William: Fair enough.

Terence: In a further ventilation of this entrancing logic, we would also have to argue that the cessation from works of penance of the majority of Catholic faithful, in spite of Our Lord's *first words* being "Do penance and believe in the Gospel,"[2] has *nothing to do* with the removal of mandatory Friday abstinence and daily Lenten fasting; it's just the fault of the lazy faithful, who should have hit upon creative penances instead of following what their forefathers had done for centuries.

William: One would have to be an idiot to think so, I'm afraid.

---

1. In *Sic et Non*, the early scholastic author Peter Abelard compiled quotations from the Church Fathers in which they appeared to contradict one another on many important topics.
2. Mark 1:15.

Terence: When all is said and done, the Novus Ordo's hyperultra-montanist defenders sound increasingly naïve, threadbare, unconvincing, disconnected from reality. Their arguments in defense of this patchwork product are an insult to the God who created reason and elevated it by His grace, who fashioned our Catholic liturgy over the ages by the breath of His Spirit, who placed on our shoulders the sweet yoke of obedience to His commandments and the light burden of submission to His Providence.

William: I hope you're not including me among these defenders!

Terence: No, you have a great deal of common sense, which has served you well in these horrid times.

William: What do you think Catholics ought to do, then?

Terence: For God's sake (truly), let us put aside forced apologetics for the liturgical reform, see it unflinchingly for the stupendous disaster it was, and seek our healing in a return to venerable rites hallowed by centuries of faith and devotion. As a matter of fact, these rites never perished—they were not allowed by God to perish!—and today they are taking root in more and more places, as true nourishment for a flock reprehensibly neglected.

William: And what are the implications for the pope? After all, it was the papacy that started this whole conversation...

Terence: When Jesus said solemnly to Peter: "Feed my sheep . . . feed my lambs,"[3] He was *asking* him to take that task upon himself. He was not stating "You *will* feed my sheep and lambs," as if he would automatically do it, whether he wanted to or not! Every pope—indeed, every spiritual shepherd—has to give ear to Our Lord and freely choose to follow Him, lovingly feeding the sheep and lambs purchased by His Precious Blood. May our shepherds awaken, if they have not already done so, to the urgent need to restore to full

3. John 21:15–19.

honor and magnificence the traditional worship of the Church, which should never have been despised and set aside.

William: Whatever differences remain between us, Terry, we definitely agree on that.

11

"The Glue that Holds
All of Catholicism Together"

An Interview with Aurelio Porfiri

What prompted you to write your book?[1]

The liturgy of the Church is the font and apex of her entire life. Through it, in the highest, most public, most solemn way, we give honor, glory, praise, adoration, and thanksgiving to God, who is worthy of all of our love. Through it, we express our repentance and our joy, our neediness and our longing for Him. In it we find the Word of God in the splendor of His holy ones, the pearl of great price and the one thing needful, the Bread of Angels, the foretaste of heaven. There is nothing that comes even close to it in importance.

And yet—everywhere the liturgy is in shambles. It is badly celebrated, with scandalous contempt for the sacred. There is vast ignorance of the great Latin tradition, when there is not active hostility towards it. The diseases of individualism, utilitarianism, and minimalism have settled into every part of the body like a wasting cancer. The liturgy is in an almost perpetual state of abuse. That which is most precious, most pure, most holy, and most sanctifying has become an abomination of desolation.

This situation moves me to anguish, indignation, and zeal, as it does anyone who wishes to serve the Lord in the "beauty of holiness." I want to do something about it, so, following the Benedictine

---

1. *Resurgent in the Midst of Crisis: Sacred Liturgy, the Traditional Latin Mass, and Renewal in the Church* (Kettering, OH: Angelico Press, 2014).

motto *ora et labora*, I pray and I work. Writing is a big part of that work.

In the first chapter you say that solemnity is the crux of the matter. What do you mean?

There are many liturgical issues that people can discuss and debate: language, music, vestments, ceremonial, posture or stance. But it seems to me that there is a fundamental issue underlying everything else, namely, whether one approaches the sacred mysteries with genuine humility, reverence, and awe. This inner attitude is the origin of solemnity, that is, the treating of holy things *as* holy, the treating of serious things *as* serious, the treating of awesome things *as* awesome.

This solemnity is a quality that permeates the entire liturgy in its overall character as well as its tiny details. When it is absent, nothing is right. When it is present, almost any other lack can be tolerated—a poor church, a vestment that's a bit shabby, off-key singing. We would obviously prefer to have a glorious church, magnificent vestments, and wonderful sacred music, but if the spirit of solemnity is absent, none of these things can make up for it. I have been present at a humble Low Mass in a makeshift environment and have been carried up to heaven on wings of desire and contemplation by the spirit in which it was offered. I have seen a grandiose liturgy on which heaps of money and effort were expended, but because it was a man-made and man-centered show, it was a waste.

Solemnity comes from recognizing that liturgy is, if I could put it this way, a formalized wrestling with Almighty God, who is all-powerful, righteous, and glorious, a searcher of minds and hearts. It is the key "ingredient," if you will, to all good liturgy.

What is the relationship between liturgy and poverty? Should liturgy be "of the poor and for the poor," as some people say?

Following on what I said about solemnity, liturgy has to be poor in the sense that we do not bring ourselves, our egotism, to it, and fill it with our cheap goods. We must not "enrich" it out of our own brains, trying to make it "modern" and "relevant" and "creative." Rather, we must receive gratefully the treasure given to us by our Lord, His apostles, and the many standard-bearers of a long tradition that comes to us. The wealth belongs not to us but to the Church, who lends it to us for our enrichment. As in the parable, we must give it back with interest, having leveraged its own value.

Let me put it this way: liturgy in its inward spirit and its outward expression should be unspeakably *rich*, but with the riches of our Lord Jesus Christ and the mysteries of His life, death, and resurrection. He is the one who should obviously be the principal agent and the ultimate point of any liturgy. All of the liturgy's "externals" should point strongly towards Him, and through Him, to the Father. We have a mystery cult, so to speak, and it must *remain* such. This isn't what we usually find in the mainstream Catholic world, where the Mass has become a noisy, distracting, superficial, and even vulgar affair, full of verbosity from one end to the other, lacking in poetry, nobility, symbolism, and silence.

You say the crisis of the post-council is linked to the crisis of the liturgy. In what ways?

This is certainly not my insight, but that of Joseph Ratzinger and many others, like Michael Davies, who saw that the liturgical reform was the "Trojan Horse" by which modernism, liberalism, relativism, and a host of other evils entered the Church. Although in certain countries or populations Catholicism was already weakening in the 1950's, in most places and in most respects it was growing, and it could have continued to grow (with the usual bumps of fallen human life) for decades to come, if the Council had not been taken as a proclamation that all-encompassing change was overdue, that change is always good, and that we must change to accommodate and assimilate the modern world. The liturgical reform is exactly where these ideas found their most complete acceptance, their most stunning realization, and their most devastating consequences.

The Church's liturgy, though subject to ecclesiastical supervision, was always treated as a sacrosanct reality that must not be touched with profane hands. It is not our possession to do with as we please;

it is entrusted to us as a gift to love, honor, and transmit to future generations. When the old liturgy of centuries, indeed millennia, was suddenly dismantled and reconfigured in modern guise as a slim and sleek vehicle for the emerging Space Age, the defining "taboo" of the Catholic Church had been shattered. Predictably, millions of the faithful abandoned the Church: if this is how the most holy things are treated, can there be any truth at all in what the Church says? If the Holy Mass is subject to human manipulation, why not other practices that are obviously less sacred? Why not change morality to bring it up to date, or rewrite doctrine in light of Modern Thought?

Other Catholics stayed on, of course, but had to be "re-educated" to accept a new vision and a new set of priorities, which were largely at odds with what the Church had always taught and lived by. The hemorrhaging of priests and religious accelerated. Integral Catholic social teaching was abandoned—ever heard of "the social kingship of Christ"? Philosophy and theology collapsed into a balkanized war zone of competing ideologies.

The liturgy is the glue that holds all of Catholicism together, the key that keeps the other pieces in place. When it fell, everything else came apart. And wherever it returns, the fullness of Catholicism is not far behind—including Catholic culture, with the liberal arts and the fine arts. I have seen this dynamic play out many times in my lifetime, and in both directions: from disorder to order, and from order to disorder.

In one place you talk about "word versus wordiness." What is the difference?

I use this contrast to get at the distinction between *verbal* worship, which all Christian worship necessarily is, and *verbose* worship, which is antithetical to the spirit of the liturgy. As Ratzinger shows, the defining feature of our prayer is that it comes from and returns to the *Logos*. But this *Logos* is the infinite, transcendent, eternal *Logos* of God, so our prayer, too, should reflect these attributes in some way, if it is to be a faithful reflection and communicator of this Word.

"The Glue that Holds All of Catholicism Together"

A single Gregorian chant, let us say a Gradual between the readings, more profoundly conveys the *Logos* than hours of readings, homilies, lectures, or catechisms. A few minutes of adoring silence during the Canon of the Mass conveys the *Logos* more profoundly than the entire content of the Oxford English Dictionary. As a society we are addicted to words, images, and sounds, but we have forgotten their origin and their purpose.

The language of liturgy is *elevated* speech, namely, song and silence. These fraternal twins bring peace, that is, the tranquility of order; they bring contemplation, which is a foretaste of the beatific vision; they bring unity to our scattered thoughts and our broken lives. The wordiness of fallen human beings—encouraged, alas, by the rubric "in these or similar words" of the neo-Roman missal, as well as its openings for commentary and announcements—does not bring peace, contemplation, and unity.

You use an interesting phrase: you say that "the Reform has failed the Council." Can you expand on this point?

Well, sometimes I think I have been too positive about the Council in my book, and too positive about some aspects of the liturgical reform, which was, overall, a failure, as we can see in a thousand ways.

However, what I meant is that, if we take John XXIII's intentions for the Council at their face value, and if we look at much of what the documents actually say, we find a rather different picture of Catholicism than what you will find on the street. Reading the Dogmatic Constitution on the Church *Lumen Gentium* can be quite an eye-opener: one finds much traditional teaching that is absent from the consciousness of the contemporary Catholic.

The same thing is true of the Constitution on the Sacred Liturgy *Sacrosanctum Concilium*. In spite of the fact that the document was drafted and filled with loopholes by those who wished to subvert the liturgy, we find in it passages that sound shockingly "traditional" nowadays—perhaps this was the sugar-coating of the bitter pill, but still, they are actually *there*. The Mass and the Divine Office, so the document says, are supposed to remain mostly in Latin; Gregorian chant is to have chief place within the liturgy; the faithful are to learn to say and sing together *in Latin* the parts of the Mass that belong to them; the chalice is to be given to the faithful on *rare* occasions; there should be no mixing of liturgical roles; and so forth.

If this is what the Council Fathers wanted, as signified by their nearly-unanimous vote (including Archbishop Lefebvre's), then it is hard to see how the Novus Ordo Missae, the various sacramental rites, the Liturgy of the Hours, the Book of Blessings, and so forth, as we have them, correspond at all to their intentions or to their approved final document. In this sense, there can be no question that the Reform failed the Council.

This explains why there's a "reform of the reform" movement: it's rather obvious that the reform has to be reformed. But the progressive establishment has succeeded in convincing most people not only that the reform is faithful to Vatican II's dictates but also that it is the perfect embodiment of the very essence of the Council. As such, it has a status that is well-nigh unquestionable, untouchable. We have been reminded of that attitude in "Sarahgate" (as Father Hunwicke calls it).[2]

Do you consider yourself a Catholic traditionalist? And if so, what do you think the term means?

Yes, by all means! A traditionalist is one who sees the Faith, in its inner structure, as something handed down to us, not something we invent, assess, and re-create by our own lights. It is an organic set of ideas, practices, and attitudes that give birth to a culture of faith.

---

2. In an address delivered on July 5, 2016 at the Sacra Liturgia conference in London, Robert Cardinal Sarah urged priests and bishops to start celebrating Masses *ad orientem* beginning on the first Sunday of Advent that year. However, after a private meeting between Cardinal Sarah and Pope Francis on July 9, Father Federico Lombardi issued a statement on July 11 stating that Sarah's proposal was not to be taken as authoritative, that Mass should by preference be celebrated *versus populum*, that the Ordinary Form was not to be supplanted by the Extraordinary Form, and that the expression "reform of the reform" was to be avoided. Fr Hunwicke wrote about this incident at his weblog *Fr Hunwicke's Mutual Enrichment* on July 15 and July 21, 2016.

The traditionalist sees things as being irreducibly complex and necessarily bound up with the path of the Church through all the ages. He will not play time-travel games by pretending to go back to antiquity to do what the early Christians did, nor will he race ahead into futuristic realms to go where no man has gone before. He lives in the present but is rooted firmly and deeply in the past, the centuries brooded over by the Holy Spirit.

This is the Catholic Faith as all of its great fathers, doctors, and confessors have understood it and professed it and lived it. In short, a traditionalist utterly rejects the Darwinian/Hegelian view of doctrinal and liturgical development, whereby a fish becomes a fowl.

In these days there has been a lot of talk about the orientation of the priest during the Mass because of the "exchange" between Cardinal Sarah and the Vatican. What is your opinion about this?

The great liturgist Msgr Klaus Gamber once said that the turning around of the altar and the celebrant was the single worst change that happened after the Council, because it fundamentally altered people's perception of what the Mass *is*. It is first and foremost the supreme sacrifice of the Cross, in which we are permitted to participate. It is not a re-enactment of the Last Supper or a fellowship meal.

Ever since he became Prefect of the Congregation for Divine Worship and the Discipline of the Sacraments, Cardinal Sarah has been an outspoken proponent of recovering the traditional eastward stance of the celebrant at Holy Mass. He recognizes the common-sense principle that actions speak louder than words. If worship is directed to God, and if it is expressed in bodily actions and postures, the entire community—including the ministers at the altar—should be facing the same direction, towards the east. The difference this makes is enormous. Suddenly the liturgy is not the "closed circle" that Cardinal Ratzinger lamented;[3] it opens out onto the cosmos, salvation history, and eternity.

The slur about the priest "turning his back on the people" was started up *after* the Council in order to promote a certain humanis-

---

3. *The Spirit of the Liturgy*, 80–81.

tic agenda. No one ever thought of it that way before. As a wise man once said, would you want your bus driver or airplane pilot to be facing *you*, or facing *forwards*? We are on pilgrimage together; we are not a cozy, closed circle of chums.

It's not rocket science: the priest and the people are facing in the same direction, towards the Lord. That is the meaning it has always had. The moment one experiences *ad orientem* worship, and lets the mystery of the sacrifice take hold of the mind and heart, the stance becomes not only totally obvious but also deeply prayerful. It is a potent symbol of the Mass being about the adoration of God and not about us: *we* are called to worship *Him* in spirit and in truth.

The "clarifications" and "corrections" offered to Cardinal Sarah's position rely on palpably false interpretations of both the *General Instruction of the Roman Missal* and the Missal itself. The problem with GIRM 299 has been addressed by many, and as for the modern missal, an article I wrote at *New Liturgical Movement* demonstrates that it presupposes *ad orientem* as normative.[4] I also gave a talk at Silverstream Priory that goes further into the theology of *ad orientem*, for those who would like to learn more about the massive theological and spiritual implications of this matter.[5]

What is your opinion of Pope Francis?

I mentioned earlier the false view of development of doctrine. It seems to me that this card is being played nowadays over and over again: "our understanding of *x* is evolving, therefore, in the maturity of our age of the world, we can arrive at conclusions contrary to those that were once taught." Shades of Teilhard de Chardin in one respect, George Orwell in another. Pieper has a book called *Abuse of Language, Abuse of Power*. I think this is what is happening before our very eyes. The *Logos* was not respected in the liturgical realm, and now it is not respected in the doctrinal realm either.

---

4. "The Normativity of *Ad Orientem* Worship According to the Ordinary Form's Rubrics," *New Liturgical Movement*, November 23, 2015.
5. "The Sacrifice of Praise and the Ecstatic Orientation of Man," the text of which was published at *Rorate Caeli* on July 28, 2016.

I see very difficult times ahead, far more difficult than anything Catholics have had to deal with for centuries. We are at the beginning of a new "post-council" phase that will be bigger and uglier than anything that came in the wake of 1965.

Pope Francis has elevated the liturgical celebration in honor of Saint Mary Magdalene to the status of being a Feast. How do you feel about that?

As Gregory DiPippo pointed out at *New Liturgical Movement,*[6] the feast of St Mary Magdalene was traditionally given great honor and celebrated at a higher rank than one would have expected. She was venerated as "the apostle to the apostles" and had many proper Masses throughout the diverse liturgical uses of Europe. It was none other than the Bugnini team that *demoted* the status of Mary Magdalene in the 1962 *Missale Romanum.* So, in this respect, Francis is restoring things to where they ought to be. It's a curious example of an anti-Bugnini move—not that the liturgical establishment recognizes it as such or cares to know it.

On the other hand, surely Francis knew that this would be *interpreted* as a feminist move, as a sop to the proponents of women's ordination, etc., and did it anyway. One could certainly wonder about the wisdom of such a move *at this time* and with the environment we live in. And with the relative paucity of feasts in the new calendar, it gives Mary Magdalene a pronouncedly special status which may not, all things considered, exactly parallel her honorable standing in pre-Bugnini missals. As with the changes to the rule about the washing of the feet of men on Holy Thursday, we see decisions that, far from confirming the brethren in the faith, only increase the ecclesiastical confusion that surrounds us.

How does composing fit into your life as a Catholic and a liturgist?

---

6. Gregory DiPippo, "Feast of St Mary Magdalene Upgraded to Feast," *New Liturgical Movement,* June 10, 2016; cf. *idem,* "'Apostle of the Apostles'—Liturgical Notes on the Feast of St Mary Magdalene," *New Liturgical Movement,* July 22, 2018.

Composing has always been for me a way of withdrawing inwards, listening for an ideal beauty and trying to pursue it, since it is always elusive. When the work is done, I can offer it to the Lord as a little gift to the Church's treasury, and this brings me joy.

12

Recent Profane Novelties

Brother Macarius (with some animation): Father!

Brother Jonas (startled): My son, what ever is the matter?

Br. Macarius: Have you heard the news?

Br. Jonas: You know how little news enters these hallowed walls. I have heard no more than the monastic bell today—and my grumbling stomach.

Br. Macarius: The pope gave a speech about the death penalty, saying it is always and everywhere wrong—it is intrinsically evil! And that we should modify the text of the *Catechism* so that it says so![1]

Br. Jonas: One might almost be grateful that he considers *anything* intrinsically evil, after the *Amoris Laetitia* debacle. It reminds me a little of what someone once said about Marcial Maciel: "At least they were women."

Br. Macarius: You seem to be making light of a serious matter, Father.

1. Reference is made here to Pope Francis's Address to Participants in the Meeting Promoted by the Pontifical Council for Promoting the New Evangelization, October 11, 2017. This text was subsequently cited in the same pope's alteration of the *Catechism of the Catholic Church*, signed on May 11, 2018 and released on August 1.

Br. Jonas: No, no, I'm not, really. It's just that I can't be surprised anymore about the flow of bad news from Rome. When you have Honorius, Liberius, John XXII, and Paul VI all wrapped up in one modernist Jesuit from South America, what do you expect?

Br. Macarius: What's astonishing is how clearly his position goes against Divine Revelation and the Magisterium. You know the texts as well as I do: "If anyone sheds the blood of man, by man shall his blood be shed; for in the image of God has man been made."[2] "The Lord said to Moses, 'Say to the people of Israel, Any man of the people of Israel, or of the strangers that sojourn in Israel, who gives any of his children to Molech shall be put to death; the people of the land shall stone him with stones.'"[3]

Br. Jonas: Don't forget the remarkable passage in Deuteronomy: "That prophet or that dreamer of dreams shall be put to death, because he has taught rebellion against the Lord your God. . . . You shall not yield to him or listen to him, nor shall your eye pity him, nor shall you spare him, nor shall you conceal him; but you shall kill him; your hand shall be first against him to put him to death, and afterwards the hand of all the people. You shall stone him to death with stones, because he sought to draw you away from the Lord your God, who brought you out of the land of Egypt, out of the house of bondage."[4]

Br. Macarius: Not to mention the time when Jesus says: "For God commanded, 'Honor your father and your mother,' and, 'He who speaks evil of father or mother, let him surely die.'"[5]

Br. Jonas: Well, one could take that last bit figuratively, as referring to the death of the soul in mortal sin. A clearer example is when Our Lord says to Pontius Pilate, precisely concerning the death sentence:

2. Genesis 9:5–6.
3. Leviticus 20:1–2.
4. Deuteronomy 13:5, 8–10.
5. Matthew 15:4.

"You would have no power over me unless it had been given you from above; therefore he who delivered me to you has the greater sin."[6] He speaks of "sin" because Jesus was, of course, entirely innocent and therefore could never have deserved the death meted out to a notorious criminal.

Br. Macarius: And St Paul, writing to the Romans, told them expressly: "Would you have no fear of him who is in authority? Then do what is good, and you will receive his approval, for he is God's servant for your good. But if you do wrong, be afraid, for he does not bear the sword in vain; he is the servant of God to execute his wrath on the wrongdoer."[7]

Br. Jonas: Honestly, has there ever been any doubt in the minds of Catholics, in the long history of the Church, that God has commanded the death penalty in some situations? That he has given human rulers authority to use it for malefactors? That it is not only a permitted form of enacting justice but can even be the preferable one? A person would have to be…

Br. Macarius: …a heretic to deny it? Yes, quite so.

Br. Jonas: We can always disagree about when capital punishment should be used, and even whether it is "safe," if I could put it that way, for a given regime or society to have recourse to it—John Paul II raised some searching questions along these lines, regarding the callous attitude towards life and death in liberal secular governments. But none of this amounts to saying that it is intrinsically evil.

Br. Macarius: Well, just listen to what Pope Francis said in this speech he gave. I've got it printed out here. "It must be clearly stated that the death penalty is an inhumane measure that, regardless of how it is carried out, abases human dignity. It is *per se* contrary to the Gospel, because it entails the willful suppression of a human life

---

6. John 19:11.
7. Romans 13:3–4.

that never ceases to be sacred in the eyes of its Creator and of which—ultimately—only God is the true judge and guarantor."

Br. Jonas: Jumping Jesuits! How can he reconcile that with what his predecessor Pius XII taught in 1952? "Even when it is a question of the execution of a condemned man, the State does not dispose of the individual's right to life. In this case it is reserved to the public power to deprive the condemned person of the enjoyment of life in expiation of his crime when, by his crime, he has already disposed himself of his right to live."[8] And there are many other texts like this one.

Br. Macarius: Here's where it gets worse: Pope Francis actually *says* that his teaching is a novelty, and that this doesn't matter—because Christianity is going to bring forth novelties from time to time, when, I guess, people have... I don't know... matured enough?

Br. Jonas: Sounds to me like old-fashioned progressivism. The Age of Aquarius and all that! Jacques Maritain on steroids.

Br. Macarius: You said it. Listen to this bit from the speech: "It is not enough to find a new language in which to articulate our perennial faith; it is also urgent, in the light of the new challenges and prospects facing humanity, that the Church be able to express the 'new things' of Christ's Gospel, that, albeit present in the word of God, have not yet come to light."[9]

Br. Jonas: Ah, "new things"! Haven't we had enough of those in the past fifty years?

Br. Macarius: Enough and to spare.

---

8. Pope Pius XII, "The Moral Limits of Medical Research and Treatment," Address to the First International Congress on the Histopathology of the Nervous System, September 14, 1952.

9. Pope Francis, Address, October 11, 2017.

Br. Jonas: We were just talking about Pius XII, right? He said something in 1954, on the occasion of the canonization of St Pius X, that doesn't sit well with the words of our yerba mate aficionado. He said this to a large group of cardinals, archbishops, and bishops:

> If there are any present-day teachers making every effort to produce and develop new ideas, but not to repeat "that which has been handed down," and if this is their whole aim, they should reflect calmly on those words which Benedict XV proposes for their consideration: "We wish this maxim of our elders held in reverence: *Nihil innovetur nisi quod traditum*—let nothing new be introduced, but only what has been handed down; it must be held as an inviolable law in matters of faith, and should also control those points which allow of change, though in these latter for the most part the rule holds: *non nova sed noviter*—not new things but in a new way."[10]

Br. Macarius: The death penalty's legitimacy is clearly not one of those things that can change.

Br. Jonas: Of course not. Not in itself. Its actual employment can change according to circumstances, but not the inherent right of the political authority to use it.

Br. Macarius: Yes. And adding duplicity to innovation, Pope Francis cites a few lines from John XXIII's opening speech of October 11, 1962, to the Second Vatican Council—but *not* those lines that undermine Francis's agenda. Articulating the purpose of the Council, John XXIII stated:

> What instead is necessary today is that the whole of Christian doctrine, with no part of it lost, be received in our times by all with a new fervor, in serenity and peace, in that traditional and precise conceptuality and expression which is especially displayed in the acts of the Councils of Trent and Vatican I. As all sincere promoters of Christian, Catholic, and apostolic faith strongly desire, what

---

10. Pope Pius XII, *Si Diligis*, Allocution to Cardinals, Archbishops, and Bishops on the Occasion of the Canonization of St Pius X, May 31, 1954.

is needed is that *this* doctrine[11] be more fully and more profoundly known, and that minds be more fully imbued and formed by it. What is needed is that this certain and unchangeable doctrine, to which loyal submission is due, be investigated and presented in the way demanded by our times…

Br. Jonas: …and I can finish off that famous part with the line everyone quotes: "For the deposit of faith, the truths contained in our venerable doctrine, are one thing; the manner in which they are expressed, but with the same meaning and the same judgment, is another thing." This is classic stuff.

Br. Macarius: Some people question whether you can so easily separate the truths of doctrine from their formulations. If you say something in a way that is *too* new, you risk altering the meaning and judgment, don't you think? We've certainly seen that happen with the liturgy. Changing the *lex orandi* has effectively, for most Catholics, changed the *lex credendi*.

Br. Jonas: No doubt that's true. But it's obvious, isn't it, that Pius XII and John XXIII are just expressing the undisputed and indisputable view of St Vincent of Lérins? You remember what that great Father of the Church says:

> The Church of Christ, the careful and watchful guardian of the doctrines deposited in her charge, never changes anything in them, never diminishes, never adds, does not cut off what is necessary, does not add what is superfluous, does not lose her own, does not appropriate what is another's, but while dealing faithfully and judiciously with ancient doctrine, keeps this one object carefully in view—if there be anything which antiquity has left shapeless and rudimentary, to fashion and polish it, if anything already reduced to shape and developed, to consolidate and strengthen it, if anything already ratified and defined, to keep and guard it.[12]

11. Emphasis added.
12. Vincent, *Commonitory*, ch. 23.

And he says that sometimes the Church will "designate an old article of the faith by the characteristic of a new name, for better understanding."

Br. Macarius: The clarity and logic, the vigor and zeal of St Vincent! How we need this again in our day. His treatise is endlessly quotable. Here's one of my favorite passages:

> I cannot sufficiently wonder at the madness of certain men, at the impiety of their blinded understanding, at their lust of error, such that, not content with the rule of faith delivered once for all, and received from the times of old, they are every day seeking one novelty after another, and are constantly longing to add, change, take away, in religion, as though the doctrine, *Let what has once for all been revealed suffice*, were not a heavenly but an earthly rule—a rule which could not be complied with except by continual emendation, nay, rather by continual fault-finding.[13]

Br. Jonas: Brilliant, just brilliant. It's as if he's describing this very pontificate.

Br. Macarius: Gotta love Patristic invective. These men were no wallflowers.

Br. Jonas: That's probably why the master polemicist St Maximus the Confessor ended up having his tongue cut out and his hand cut off by that wicked emperor—I forget his name—

Br. Macarius: Constans II.

Br. Jonas: How can you remember so many details?

Br. Macarius: I think we're getting off track. Will you believe me if I tell you that Pope Francis had the gall to cite Vincent of Lérins in this speech of his?

---

13. Ibid., ch. 21.

Br. Jonas: You've got to be kidding.

Br. Macarius: No, it's only too true! He cites the beginning of chapter 23, but stops right before Vincent explains what progress actually means—and it's the opposite of what Pope Francis is doing today. You know how that amazing chapter starts: "Someone will say, perhaps, 'Shall there, then, be no progress in Christ's Church?' Certainly; all possible progress. For what being is there, so envious of men, so full of hatred to God, who would seek to forbid it?" That's the bit Bergoglio puts in—and then quotes no more.

Br. Jonas: You mean he doesn't go on with the rest?

> Yet on condition that it be real progress of faith [*profectus fidei*], not alteration [*permutatio*]. For progress requires that the subject be enlarged in itself; alteration, that it be transformed into something else. The intelligence, then, the knowledge, the wisdom, as well of individuals as of all, as well of one man as of the whole Church, ought, in the course of ages and centuries, to increase and make much and vigorous progress, yet only in its own kind—that is to say, in the same doctrine, in the same sense, and in the same meaning.

Br. Macarius: There's the famous phrase: *in eodem scilicet dogmate, eodem sensu, eademque sententia*. I wonder how many dozens of times that phrase has been quoted in papal and conciliar documents?

Br. Jonas: John Paul II used it in *Veritatis Splendor* when asserting that the Church's moral teaching could develop in its formulations but never be altered in its *sensus* and *sententia*.[14] (*Sighs*.) One misses John Paul II these days, no? After Assisi, I thought I'd never say that.

Br. Macarius: So, as I was saying, Pope Francis misuses Vincent. Both citations of the *Commonitory* in his speech give the reader a false understanding of what Vincent is saying—a technique Vincent

---

14. John Paul II, Encyclical Letter *Veritatis Splendor* (August 6, 1993), n. 53.

himself critiques in chapter 7 of his treatise, "How heretics craftily cite obscure passages in ancient writers in support of their own novelties."

Br. Jonas: Where does that leave us, young man?

Br. Macarius: Pope Francis is telling us that, after 2,000 years of Christians accepting and defending capital punishment on the basis of divine revelation and sound philosophical reasoning, we are now in a position to see that it was intrinsically evil all along. He is uttering sheer novelty, in the worst sense of the word.

Br. Jonas: I see. Is he not, then, espousing the idea that there can be not only new statements of doctrines already held by Christians, but actually *new doctrines* in Christianity? This flies directly in the face of the Church's self-understanding from St Peter down to Benedict XVI.

Br. Macarius: Exactly. As the Apostle perfectly summed it up: "I delivered to you as of first importance what I also received."[15]

Br. Jonas: He said it more than once, too: "I commend you because you remember me in everything and maintain the traditions even as I have delivered them to you."[16]

Br. Macarius: Don't forget this one: "So then, brethren, stand firm and hold to the traditions which you were taught by us, either by word of mouth or by letter."[17]

Br. Jonas: This is why Benedict XVI was so adamant that a pope does not make up the Faith. He does not pull rabbits out of hats—or should I say, doves out of tiaras?

15. 1 Corinthians 15:3.
16. 1 Corinthians 11:2.
17. 2 Thessalonians 2:15.

Br. Macarius: The sanity of Ratzinger! "The First Vatican Council had in no way defined the pope as an absolute monarch. On the contrary, it presented him as the guarantor of obedience to the revealed Word. The pope's authority is bound to the tradition of faith. . . . The authority of the pope is not unlimited; it is at the service of Sacred Tradition."[18]

Br. Jonas: Or when he said: "The pope knows that in his important decisions, he is bound to the great community of faith of all times, to the binding interpretations that have developed throughout the Church's pilgrimage. Thus, his power is not being above the Word of God, but at the service of it. It is incumbent upon him to ensure that this Word continues to be present in its greatness and to resound in its purity, so that it is not torn to pieces by continuous changes in usage."[19]

Br. Macarius: Would that Benedict XVI's words were being followed today, rather than trampled underfoot like so much rubbish!

Br. Jonas: The Lord will win in His good time; we just have to be patient. The days of Francis are numbered. The reaction against him will be powerful, you wait and see.

Br. Macarius: I know you are right, but I was still so upset by this death penalty speech.

Br. Jonas: Just because of how flagrantly it contradicts Scripture and Tradition?

Br. Macarius: Well, yes—but it's even worse than that. The implications of Pope Francis's speech are staggering.

Br. Jonas: You've always had a sharper theological mind than I. Can you help me see those implications?

18. Ratzinger, *Spirit of the Liturgy*, 166.
19. Benedict XVI, Homily, May 7, 2005.

Br. Macarius: First, we know that God commanded the Israelites in the Old Testament to use the death penalty. Therefore, God commanded them to perform intrinsically evil acts. Second, we know too that the New Testament speaks favorably of capital punishment. Therefore, our inspired authors accepted, and taught, that intrinsically evil acts are legitimate. Finally, countless popes and councils throughout Church history accepted and taught the acceptability of capital punishment. Therefore, the universal ordinary magisterium of the Church accepted and taught that intrinsically evil acts should be performed.

Br. Jonas: Can any of these conclusions be uttered without blasphemy!?

Br. Macarius: Such confusion is characteristic of this papacy, for at the same time Francis has taken adultery off the table as an intrinsically evil act, in spite of the explicit condemnation of it in both Testaments and in the unbroken magisterium of the Church. In keeping with trends of political correctness, the traditional mortal sins that would bar one from receiving communion are rehabilitated as "the best some people can do" (maybe most people?), while the sins recognized by European liberals, such as limiting immigration, harming the environment, and putting convicted criminals to death, are recategorized as the great moral evils of our time.

Br. Jonas: What do you think are the deeper foundations of Francis's views in this speech? I mean, what is driving him?

Br. Macarius: It is hard to say. There are a number of possible explanations.

Br. Jonas: I'm all ears, but don't go too fast or you'll lose me.

Br. Macarius: Maybe Francis holds to an Ockhamist voluntarism whereby what is good or evil depends merely on God's whim. There is no eternal right and wrong for human nature that man can glimpse with his reason and receive definitively from revelation...

Br. Jonas: …and so, what is right and wrong will change depending on what the "God of surprises" has in store for us next, as declared through his appointed mouthpiece on earth.

Br. Macarius: Or maybe Francis holds that God commands (or allows?) people to do evil things because He knows that these evil things are "the best they can do for now." Thus, the ancient Israelites killing Canaanites, or medieval Catholics killing heretics, are morally equivalent to divorced men and women of the modern West engaging in sexual relations with someone other than their original spouse.

Br. Jonas: You mean, in each case it is the best that can be expected at this person's stage of moral development?

Br. Macarius: Right. Again, perhaps Francis holds that part of man's moral progress over the centuries is to come to the realization that certain things God told him were good are actually evil, and so he needs to "correct" God's revelation by his own superior wisdom; and that things God told him were evil are actually permissible, once again requiring a correction of the narrowness of a legalistic God by the breadth of human compassion. In this Hegelian view, God and man evolve together: our reasonings, our social perceptions, our feelings, *are* part of the unfolding of divine law.

Br. Jonas: Raving lunacy!

Br. Macarius: It sure is. Another version of the last view is that the God of the Old Testament has been superseded by the God of the New Testament, and that the God of the New Testament has been superseded by the God of Modernity. It is Marcionism with a twist—for now we find that it was not only the bloodthirsty Yahweh of olden times who was hiding from us the true face of the merciful God, but even the highly-demanding Jesus, whose moral law is far more demanding than that of Moses.

Br. Jonas: This last phase, too, has to be superseded if we are to enter the Age of Mercy.

Br. Macarius: Or the Age of Something.

Br. Jonas: I remember a Scripture course I had back in college. It was taught by a devotee of the historical-critical method who maintained that much of what Scripture attributed to God or to Christ was made up by the authors and therefore could not be said to be divinely authorized. And it was the job of the Scripture scholar to sort out what things are genuine and what things are fake.

Br. Macarius: Indeed, it's quite a popular approach, and one can see why: Scripture can be made to say, or not say, anything you like. So, Francis might believe that God never commanded the Jews to use the death penalty in the first place, and that Jesus never actually taught His disciples that remarrying after divorce was adultery. The Jews *wanted* to kill people, so they attributed their views to God. Some early Christian rigorists *wanted* Jesus to say these things about divorce and adultery, so they put the words in His mouth.

Br. Jonas: And let me guess—we know (somehow) that the real Jesus would never have said such harsh, judgmental, unloving, and off-putting things. St Paul, who was a Jewish-trained rigorist, developed a moral theology that was radically different from the plain teaching of the nature-loving, fun-loving, "to understand all is to forgive all" proto-hippie Jesus of Nazareth. Francis is taking us back beyond the grimy build-up of a 2,000-year-old Pharisaical hijacking of the original Gospel message. How liberating!

Br. Macarius: Don't forget your guitar and your bong.

Br. Jonas: This *is* all rather disturbing, especially when it's coming from a member of the clergy—let alone the Roman Pontiff! I can see why you were agitated.

Br. Macarius: I feel better, though, talking it over with you. Somehow seeing the evil for what it is galvanizes me to fight against it in prayer, in monastic obedience, in offering up my sufferings, and in doing what I can to give good counsel to our guests, who invariably ask about these things.

Br. Jonas (pauses): I've often wondered how much of this current crisis can be traced back to the Second Vatican Council itself.

Br. Macarius: That's a huge question, and we're running out of time before Vespers. Why don't we take it up another day?

Br. Jonas: All right. Sufficient for the day are the evils thereunto.

Br. Macarius: But I do have one last thought to share with you, which touches somewhat on that topic. Several of the blasphemous positions I summarized might be seen together as a new form of Joachimism, whereby we are now living, after the Second Vatican Council, in the Age of the Spirit, which goes as far beyond the Age of the Son—represented by Church councils, canon laws, rubrics, and precepts—as the Age of the Son went beyond the Age of the Father, with its animal sacrifices, ritual ablutions, and priestly caste. This new Age of the Spirit is characterized above all by the goodness of everyone and everything...

Br. Jonas: ... except of those who deny the goodness of everyone and everything.

Br. Macarius: They, of course, would be the false prophets that must arise whenever the Spirit of newness is poured out with new fullness.

Br. Jonas: Ah, there's all that newness again! All I can say is, I don't want a new Spirit; I want the Holy Spirit, with the fullness He poured into the Church on the day of Pentecost. The eternal newness of Christ, "the same yesterday and today and for ever."[20]

Br. Macarius: There is only *one* Spirit and *one* Pentecost. Anything

20. Hebrews 13:8.

else is a lying spirit. I was thinking of one of the more interesting features of the Montanist schism in the early Church, namely, their claim that divine revelation was, in their day, still in process. In other words, revelation was an internal "charismatic" phenomenon, no longer to be identified with the apostolic *depositum fidei*.

Br. Jonas: That very Montanist thesis, under the guise of "development," is precisely what is being imposed upon us today. To resist it is to be guilty of "grieving the Holy Spirit." What humbug!

Br. Macarius: I take it, then, you're in favor of "the antiquity and universality of the Catholic Faith against the profane novelties of all heresies," as our beloved brother St Vincent of Lérins puts it.

Br. Jonas: You bet. Monks-in-arms.

Br. Macarius: Ah, that'll be the bell for Vespers.

13

"Long Before This
Brigade of -isms Muscled In"

An Interview with Aurelio Porfiri

Your book uses the phrase "noble beauty" in its title.[1] How would you describe the noble beauty of the liturgy?

There are many different kinds of beauty. There is the simple, domestic beauty we associate with well-made furniture, carpets, blankets, plates, and books. There is an austere beauty, such as one might find in the cell of a Carthusian. There is rugged beauty, such as we see in the landscapes of Iceland or Canada or Alaska. But there is a noble beauty that we associate with sovereignty, majesty, occasions of great public solemnity. The liturgy is our courtly audience with the king of heaven and earth. It should be characterized by a tremendous sense of spaciousness, elevation, dignity, and splendor. That is what I am driving at in my title.

Who is your ideal reader? How do you imagine your audience?

One reader described me as "giving old arguments new juice." I was born well after the Second Vatican Council ended and after Paul VI had already imposed a new Mass. All of the traditional things I love are things that almost went extinct. My friends and I had to stumble upon them and discover them anew. For that reason, I see it all with

---

1. *Noble Beauty, Transcendent Holiness: Why the Modern Age Needs the Mass of Ages* (Kettering, OH: Angelico, 2017).

fresh eyes: I have no nostalgic memories. My writings seem to speak especially to young people who are in the same boat. This book is largely an *apologia* for the ancient liturgy and the whole worldview it embodies—which is definitely not that of modernity.

My ideal reader? Someone who has an open mind to the proposal that past generations might have had more wisdom than we do.

You use the term "Mass of Ages" in your subtitle. Sounds a bit sentimental, doesn't it?

Well, I once thought of it that way, too. But something changed for me. My careful study of liturgical history led me to see that, in fact, the Roman Catholic liturgy—by which I mean all of the interconnected rites and uses found within Latin Christendom—is substantially one and the same over all the centuries, developing slowly and organically, until you reach the dramatic break in 1969. The core of the Mass of St Gregory the Great was still the core of the Mass of John XXIII. After Trent, St Pius V for all intents and purposes codified the papal rite of Rome that stretched far back in time and shared much in common with other Western uses. Subsequent popes received this rite as a given. It really is, therefore, the Mass of all the Catholic centuries. It is a Mass that grew to maturity over the ages and reflects all that is best in the Church's devotion and theology.

You and I wrote together a public (and successful) declaration on sacred music, regarding both forms of the Roman rite.[2] Do you think an exchange between the two forms is feasible?

Indeed, it is possible, but, as many have observed, the traffic seems to flow more easily from the old to the new. There is a certain poverty of rubric, gesture, text, and music in the new form that begs for

---

2. Here Mr Porfiri refers to *"Cantate Domino Canticum Novum"*: *A Statement on the Current Situation of Sacred Music*, which was published on March 5, 2017, the fiftieth anniversary of the 1967 Instruction *Musicam Sacram*, and signed by over 200 musicians, pastors, and scholars from around the world. It is available in 9 languages at the website altaredei.com.

an augmentation and elevation for which the liturgical heritage of the Church provides ample material. It is fairly easy to implement such improvements because of the open-ended, option-friendly design of the Novus Ordo.

The new form, on the other hand, has relatively little that it can give to the old form. The proposals people sometimes make—the new lectionary, the new calendar, the new prefaces—are all controversial in one way or another, and by no means examples of obvious improvement.

Beyond this, there is a serious practical difficulty: most proponents of the old form are shell-shocked by decades of liturgical warfare and are not at all interested in seeing any changes at this time, while most proponents of the new form are quite content with its modern features and are not hankering for (or are even downright opposed to) any input from tradition. At this time, it strikes me as a deadlock. Of course, things could change depending on who the next pope is.

In your first chapter you intend to bring us "beyond the long winter of rationalism." How?

Since the late Middle Ages and the introduction of nominalism and voluntarism, modernity has been on a crash course of ongoing simplification. Instead of a rich blend of faith and reason, we have rationalism, the attempt to reduce things to immediate comprehension. Instead of a subtle relation of human freedom and obedience to divine authority, we have liberalism, the attempt to make man's action the sole driving force. Instead of seeing the transcendent shining through and hiding within the created order, we have materialism—the attempt to escape from the perplexing demands of a God who is both imminent and transcendent, present in all things and utterly beyond them.

These and similar trends of thinking have powerfully affected everything we do—including our liturgical worship. The traditional liturgical rites of the Catholic Church were born and flourished long before this brigade of -isms muscled in. They show a fundamentally different way of representing and engaging with the mystery of God, the mysteries of Christ, and the workings of the Holy

Spirit. Hence, they can rescue us from the prison of the fashions of our modern times.

Let me quote you: "Why did the liturgical reform of the 1960's and 1970's fail to produce a new springtime in the Church? What, in contrast, is the secret of the old Latin Mass's appeal—the reason or reasons for its surprising resurgence in our day, when most of the people who celebrate or attend it were born after 1970? And how is this development good for the Church and for the New Evangelization?" What is the answer?

Complicated questions have complex answers. The common critique made by many about the Second Vatican Council is that it seemed to adopt, or at least to suggest to bystanders, a model of accommodation to the modern secular world. This model strongly influenced the process of liturgical reform. But the revolution of 1968 already announced the death of the main phase of modernity, and the subsequent radical pluralism of post-modernity has not been friendly to the Catholic Church or her now-dated means of engagement.

This is why the old liturgical forms can burst on to the scene as something remarkably fresh, vital, captivating, provocative. The traditional Mass challenges our assumptions, our self-centered worldview, our conveniences; its antiquity has a weight to it that nothing in our world of planned obsolescence can hold a candle up to; its density forces us to work harder, with a greater yield; its sobriety calms us, its ritual mesmerizes us, its majesty impresses us, its orthodoxy converts us, and its palpable holiness drives us to deeper sanctity.

For all these reasons, the recovery of this pre-modern worship is crucial for the health of the post-modern Church, and for the success of her evangelization among people who are jaded, bored, and tired of the empty promises of our day.

You speak about the danger of simplicity and the attraction of complexity. What do you mean by that?

The idea that people want simple things is a Cartesian myth. I mean, sure, we want a can-opener or a click-pen that's easy to use, but when it comes to something we see as really important—great public events, athletic contests, award ceremonies, fundraising banquets, international conferences, even weddings—people still love a certain pageantry, lavishness, sophistication. And this involves a lot of planning, people, choreography, decoration, and finesse.

In the pre-modern world, the liturgy of the Church was the single greatest public event. The entire society was ordered to the worthy offering of this objective, public, formal, solemn sacrifice of praise to God, and no cost was spared. This made it a magnet for attendance. That's why I'm not surprised that today, whenever a bishop or cardinal offers a Pontifical Mass, the church is usually packed with a lot of people, the majority of whom are middle-aged or younger. The splendor of the event just makes sense: if we have the vicar of the Eternal High Priest in our midst, offering up "the full, final sacrifice" (Crashaw) that glorifies God and redeems the universe, why would we not "pull out all the stops"?

Conversely, if we simplify and strip down what we do, it will not lead to a Carthusian intensity; it will lead to empty pews as people look for religious ritual and ultimate meaning elsewhere.

This year we are celebrating the tenth anniversary of Summorum Pontificum. *There are many rumors about this document, including that of a possible change in policy toward the "Mass of Ages." Are you aware of this?*

I tend to agree with those who think that the generators of these rumors are wishful thinkers who are trying to influence opinion and push their own agenda. Since they have always disliked the *motu proprio,* they want others to dislike it and to view it under a cloud of suspicion as "the document that's soon going to be repealed." It's a classic media strategy.

But one thing is for certain: since we are living in such volatile and confusing times, the best strategy for Catholics is to remain faithful to the Church's tradition—her Scripture, her Fathers and Doctors, her time-honored orthodox liturgical rites. Or if these are unfamiliar, to get to know and love them well.

14

A Nightmare and a Dream

Brother Ildefonse: Last night I woke up from the most horrendous nightmare.

Brother Pachomius: Tell me about it, if you can remember enough.

Br. Ildefonse: It was extraordinarily vivid. Almost like a vision. I dreamt that I was in Rome and that there was a new pope. I never heard his name, but priests around me at the table were talking about various things he was doing. They said he suppressed a flourishing branch of the Franciscans, that he set up rules limiting the creation of new traditional orders, and imposed crippling conditions on contemplative sisters.

Br. Pachomius: *Quod Deus avertat!*

Br. Ildefonse: But that wasn't all, not by long shot. They were saying he had made a mockery of the ritual of washing the feet by first ignoring the rule that only men's feet should be washed, then by changing the rule itself, and finally by breaking even his new rule. He pushed through a commission on deaconesses even though the question had already been thoroughly examined. And he insulted a Cardinal by publicly rebuking him, even though all he had done was to remind everyone of fundamental symbols of Christian worship and of the existing law of the Church.

Br. Pachomius: A nightmare indeed!

Br. Ildefonse: Oh, I wish that that had been the end of it, but it went on. In order to guarantee the triumph of modernism, they said he was yanking conservative bishops from their sees on the slightest pretexts while leaving alone liberal bishops with far greater blemishes, that he was pushing "decentralization" so that episcopal bureaucracies could force their progressive agendas on unwilling bishops, that he picked some of the most notoriously liberal bishops to pick out new bishops for America in order to slow down or stop the traditional revival that's happening there.

Br. Pachomius: One wonders if the good Lord hasn't permitted the devil himself to interfere with your sleep.

Br. Ildefonse: But the worst was yet to come. This pope, apparently, had dared to lay hands on marriage itself. He changed the annulment process, letting in the secular divorce mentality. He held synods in which he destabilized public perception of Catholic teaching and the adherence of the People of God to moral doctrine. He even wrote a document that ambiguously allowed holy communion to be given to people in a state of civil remarriage who had been married as Catholics before, but without any annulment. In all these different ways, he played upon the gullibility and credulity of faithful Catholics. The result was an utter polarization among practicing Catholics: a majority who supported and defended him (or at least found ways to excuse him), and a minority who saw his plan and opposed it with all their might. The priests in whose company I found myself were among this minority.

Br. Pachomius: It is surely true that our dreams make fools of us, playthings of our imaginations. No real pope could ever be like that! You must have been reading a lot of Robert Hugh Benson lately.

Br. Ildefonse: I think there was more, too, that I'm having trouble recalling; something about changing the *Catechism* in a way that contradicted 2,000 years of Catholic tradition.

Br. Pachomius: Well, you should be grateful that your nightmare had shifted from horror into the realm of comic absurdity.

Br. Ildefonse: I can hardly tell you my sense of relief when I awoke. And it's funny you should mention Benson—as a matter of fact, I have been reading a good deal of him in the past few months. I was just thinking to myself how, in his apocalyptic novel *Lord of the World*, it is the pope who stands firm against error and evil, in the midst of a world totally hostile to the Church.

Br. Pachomius: You're right, I remember it very well. Oh, that's the bell now for Sext. After what you've recounted, we'd better ask for some *veram pacem cordium*, don't you think?

(*Sometime the following week.*)

Br. Ildefonse: Ah, dear brother, I must tell you about the most beautiful dream I had—it was as lovely as the other was (*he shivers*) distressing.

Br. Pachomius: Tell on, Father.

Br. Ildefonse: I dreamt that a black man in white robes was imparting the Urbi et Orbi blessing. Behind him was a cadre of papal gentlemen in regalia, poles mounted with peacock feathers, and silver trumpets. Then things got a bit confused, and it seemed that we were inside St Peter's Basilica. There was a grand papal ceremony taking place. The pope—it was the same person as before—announced that all Masses were to be celebrated *ad orientem* starting that Advent. He also announced that every parish in the Catholic world had to begin to offer at least one traditional Mass each Sunday. His words were greeted with thunderous applause, after which he looked up and said: "I am grateful for your support and your prayers, but please remember not to applaud in church. It is the place of mystery, of silence."

Br. Pachomius: How marvelous!

Br. Ildefonse: Then I was in the midst of a solemn papal liturgy, with more ministers than I have ever seen. The sound of the people chanting the Creed together in Latin was like the roar of mighty waters. The strains of Palestrina floated through the air at the offertorium while billowing clouds of incense rose up to the heights of Bernini's baldacchino and Michelangelo's dome. The silent canon began, and there was an intense, almost palpable sense of the Holy Spirit returning to dwell in His holy temple, from which He had been expelled. I felt as if I were standing on the threshold of the heavenly Jerusalem.

Br. Pachomius: Would it not be an immense gift from God, were such a dream to come true? Even if only part of it!

Br. Ildefonse: You're telling me. And that wasn't all. The dream shifted into another room, somewhere in the papal palaces. The pope was addressing a gathering—it looked like cardinals, bishops, patriarchs, and others, too—about new requirements he was imposing on the Church for its spiritual health. He spoke of how all clergy would be required to take the Oath against Modernism and profess the Creed of the Council of Trent, and that no priest who could not swear upon the triple ground of Scripture, Tradition, and Magisterium would ever be appointed a bishop under his pontificate. He said that the traditional principle of praying the entire psalter of 150 psalms each week, in their integrity, would soon be reinstated. There were many others things, too, that I cannot now remember—you know how it is with dreams.

Br. Pachomius: Better and better! This is a dream straight from heaven.

Br. Ildefonse: I awoke with a groan when my clock went off for Matins. My delight dissipated into the quiet darkness. But the dream had awakened in my heart a hope that God, for whom nothing is impossible, might work even such miracles for His people.

Br. Pachomius: "The arm of the Lord is not shortened," as you often say.

Br. Ildefonse: No, it certainly is not, although the Lord for His own reasons will sometimes keep His arm hidden for a long time. After all, the children of Abraham were slaves in Egypt for many generations before the Lord delivered them from bondage.

Br. Pachomius: I'm sure the children of Israel, during their seventy years of captivity in Babylon, must have thought it would never come to an end. And even when it did, not all of them wanted to return home; some preferred to stay in foreign lands. But as we know, God brought good even out of that stubbornness.

Br. Ildefonse: Yes—though I must admit I often find myself wondering just how God will bring good out of this morass of mediocrity in which we languish. It will take a pope of the stature of Gregory the Great, Gregory VII, Innocent III, Pius V, or Pius X to set the Barque of the Church back on course again. Indeed, it will take several such popes. May Our Lord in His infinite mercy grant them to us, in spite of our unworthiness.

Br. Pachomius: From your mouth to God's ear.

Br. Ildefonse: Well, it's getting to be time for Vespers. Let's be on our way.

15

"Nostalgically Stuck in the Spirit of Vatican II"

An Interview with Diane Montagna

Pope Francis wrote a public letter to Cardinal Robert Sarah, the Vatican's liturgy chief, correcting him for seeking to rein in the pope's new liturgical decentralization.[1] What in your view is the most significant aspect of Pope Francis's letter to Cardinal Sarah?

The most significant aspect by far is the rather blunt setting-aside of key provisions of *Liturgiam Authenticam*,[2] which was the fruit of years of responding to egregious difficulties and errors on the part of many vernacular translations.

The original ICEL[3] translation of the Roman Missal and other books was a pathetic travesty of the source texts and led to the entrenchment of numerous bad mental and liturgical habits. (As a bishop once said to a member of the original ICEL team: "I see the

---

1. On September 9, 2017, Pope Francis released a motu proprio entitled *Magnum Principium*, in which he restored to episcopal conferences the authority to "recognize" or approve translations of liturgical texts. On October 1, Cardinal Sarah published a commentary in which he argued that the new motu proprio did not alter the Holy See's final responsibility for approving such translations. Pope Francis addressed a letter to the cardinal, dated October 15, correcting him for having misrepresented the motu proprio's change in policy. This letter was then made public on October 22.

2. Congregation for Divine Worship and the Discipline of the Sacraments, Fifth Instruction for the Right Implementation of the Constitution on the Sacred Liturgy of the Second Vatican Council *Liturgiam Authenticam* (March 28, 2001).

3. International Commission on English in the Liturgy.

dynamism, but where's the equivalency?") The process that led to the new English translation, while certainly not perfect from any number of viewpoints, at least ensured a substantial correspondence in the *lex orandi* or law of prayer. I still notice when attending Novus Ordo Masses how much richer and more Catholic the texts are, in spite of their remaining defects in comparison with the traditional Roman Missal.

In the pope's letter to Cardinal Sarah, it is clear that the principles for which Wojtyła and Ratzinger fought are being retired or sidelined so that we can go back to the 1970's—"always backwards, never forwards" seems to be the motto of the liturgical progressives, who are nostalgically stuck in a certain "spirit of Vatican II" mentality and cannot advance beyond the narrow agenda characteristic of that phase.

Can you please explain for readers what principles of Liturgiam Authenticam *have been changed?*

Liturgiam Authenticam was an attempt to halt the balkanization and banalization of worship that had taken over in almost every language, with the exalted beauty of liturgical texts being reduced to cartoon caricatures (e.g., "he took the cup" instead of "he took this precious chalice in his holy and venerable hands"). *Liturgiam Authenticam* had maintained that it was absolutely necessary for the Holy See to retain ultimate governance over translations of liturgical books, and that the Vatican can and should have final review of the texts, with the authority to change the texts. *Magnum Principium* and this new clarification are a reversal of that long-overdue course correction.

As the Church prays, so she believes. What long-term effects could these changes have on people's faith?

When we see the phrase "legitimate adaptations," we should recognize it as code language for experimental inculturation that breaks apart the substantial unity of the Roman Rite. Indeed, this has already been done by the hundreds of vernacular translations already in existence as well as the plethora of options in the new liturgical books, but in recent moves we are seeing an acceleration of regionalism and pluralism.

The episcopal conferences already have far too much power, which has taken away from the role and responsibility of individual bishops and of the pope. It is not in keeping with the principle of subsidiarity because each bishop is supreme in his diocese, and the pope is supreme over the whole Church; episcopal conferences are mere bureaucratic mechanisms having no inherent office, authority, or responsibility. One might compare them to the United Nations in contrast to individual sovereign nations. Already at the Second Vatican Council, when some of the Fathers expressed a desire that greater authority, independent of Rome, be vested in national episcopacies, other Fathers strongly countered, saying it would fragment the Church in her expressions of faith.

More deeply, the calling into question of *Liturgiam Authenticam* (n. 80, in particular) is a continuation of the pope's novel explanation of doctrinal development, where he sets aside the perennial principle of St Vincent of Lérins, often cited by earlier popes, that whenever something new is said—and we could consider a liturgical translation to be a new thing being said—it should always be *in eodem dogmate, eodem sensu, eademque sententia*—expressing the same doctrine, the same meaning, the same judgment.

This is not at all the way progressives think about dogmatic definitions, moral teachings, or liturgical texts. All of these, for them, are permanently adaptable, changeable, even contradictable, depending on the supposed "progress" of society, culture, and mentality. It is an inherently evolutionist point of view, indebted to Hegel and Darwin, where one can get a fowl from a fish. Whether or not this is true about the natural world, it has never been believed to be true of sacred doctrine.

Dr Kwasniewski, you have written extensively on the liturgical fallout after Vatican II. What do you anticipate might be the repercussions of the pope's letter and its contents?

The invoking of "comprehension of the [liturgical] text by the recipients" risks reintroducing the kind of rationalism that has made a wasteland out of Catholic liturgy.

The liturgy, as a divine mystery and the work of God in our midst, cannot be comprehended by any man or even any angel. There are various ways *into* the liturgy, through the five senses and the intellect, and of course it should offer the faithful "handles" they can grasp in order to follow the unfolding rites. But a liturgy that aims to be simply and immediately understood is doomed to impoverishment, superficiality, and boredom. There is nothing to fascinate, bewilder, challenge, delight, or reward the participant.

In the liturgy we aspire to put on the mind of Christ, which is the work of a lifetime. We have to go through darkness and light, ideas and feelings, silence, emptiness, self-discipline, suffering, buoyed up by the rich resources of our 2,000-year old tradition. The reduction of liturgy to a commonplace, horizontal, tidy, and effortless "understanding" is the great error and scourge of the past 50 years.

On the other hand, some claim—and I do not know how strong their claim is—that the new process put into place by Pope Francis will make it more difficult to secure a new translation, because it will require the unanimous consent of an entire bishops' conference, rather than being in the hands of a steering committee working in tandem with the Congregation for Divine Worship to secure the latter's approval. If this is true, it will make local change more difficult, which is probably a good thing at this point.

Frankly, I cannot imagine the United States bishops *in general* wanting to do another translation, or a substantial modification of the current translation so soon after it was promulgated as the end result of an absurdly long process. I don't imagine we'll see changes right away. The real matter for concern, it seems to me, is how this is one more element in a larger campaign to undo the reformatory work of John Paul II and Benedict XVI, which was, in many ways, too little and too late, but is nonetheless the object of bitter hatred on the part of those who could never stomach the "conservatism" or even "traditionalism" of Wojtyła and Ratzinger.

Is there anything else you would like to add?

"Nostalgically Stuck in the Spirit of Vatican II"

As you know, Cardinal Marx said that *Magnum Principium* frees up episcopal conferences and makes *Liturgiam Authenticam* a dead letter. Cardinal Sarah publicly disagreed with Marx on this point—and now Pope Francis is transmitting the signal that he is taking the side of Marx rather than Sarah, just as he has endorsed Cardinal Kasper's position on communion for the divorced and remarried.

In this way, the pope is making it clearer all the time that he essentially stands with the German hierarchy, known to be one of the most liberal in the world, on the hot-button questions of the day.

16

A Day in the Life of a Monastery, Some Years in the Future

Father Prior: Well, the clothing of the brothers is coming up soon, and we have to finalize the names we will be giving them at the ceremony. A bumper crop this time around.

Father Subprior: There was a time when everyone would have expected to be given plain vanilla names—but not these young whippersnappers. They want a potent name, with a good bit of fire in it!

Father Prior: It's true. And I'm happy to go along with their zeal. When I think back to my callow youth, just after the Council, I can remember all those woolly monks who could only talk about the future—hope, change, social reform, Vietnam, Buddhism, and who knows what else. I also remember how they *hated* the old-fashioned names and titles. They wanted to be called Bill, Rick, Jimmy, or Ron, never "Brother" or "Father."

Father Subprior: I can hardly imagine what it must have been like.

Father Prior: Most of them left the religious life. A few stuck it out, and, if they're still alive, are now progressive dinosaurs—living fossils of the revolution. Their loyalty to a sunken ship amazes me. The whole project is sitting at the bottom of the ocean, abandoned and encrusted, but they still speak as if it was "the new springtime."

Father Subprior: Ah, yes, the new springtime that never came.

Instead, the nuclear winter, courtesy of Paolo Sesto. We are blessed, though, aren't we? There *is* a little bit of springtime, after all, in these young men who are going to pledge themselves to seek God under the *Rule* of our holy father Benedict.

Father Prior: From the world's point of view, it's as improbable as the Church's survival after the Enlightenment and the anti-clerical European revolutions. The revolutionaries thought they could kill the Church. But look at them now—six feet under, while the Church shows no signs of disappearing, even if some of her representatives are suffering dementia. This, too, shall pass.

Father Subprior: We'd better come back to the names.

Father Prior: Absolutely. Let's take up the ideas we had a few days ago and see what we think of them now.

Father Subprior: Brother Paul of the Rebuking of Peter.

Father Prior: Oh, that's priceless! We must give it to you know who.

Father Subprior: Undoubtedly. It fits him like a hand in a glove.

Father Prior: Coming to the next candidate, there are two that could work: Brother Chrodegang of the Old Calendar, or Brother Radbod of the Abundant Octaves.

Father Subprior: The way he was carrying on at recreation last February 14—"Will you be my Cyril and Methodius?"—had me in stitches, almost to the point of breaking the *Rule*. I'd have to say that Chrodegang is the way to go. It has the right amount of obscurantism.

Father Prior: And what of Wayne? Does anything leap out at you for him?

Father Subprior: Brother Severus of the Cleansing of the Temple—

no doubt about it. Though I've warned him more than once about being too hard on the kids who trade holy cards in the pews during long sermons.

Father Prior: Then we have our studious Jean Pierre. I was thinking either Brother Hilary of the Historicity of the Gospels or Brother Raymond of the Eternal Law. With his devotion to the inspiration and inerrancy of Scripture, the former seems obvious—although, come to think of it, the latter would appeal to his feisty side, as we saw when those eighteen dubia came out recently from seventy-three cardinals in response to Pope Francis II's encyclical *Delectatio Paelicis*.

Father Subprior: You've got a point there. Let's come back to that later on.

Father Prior: When it comes to Gerald, don't you think Brother Michael of the Ample Maniple would suit him to a T? I mean, just look at his reverence when he sets out the vestments in the sacristy.

Father Subprior: One day I saw him carefully spot-cleaning and pressing the maniples so that they would all be in pristine condition. And he's no less eager to clean and straighten out his soul. What about Ippolito, our resident Roman? Surely for him, a name dripping with *Romanitas* has to be found.

Father Prior: Don't you remember? We had already discussed at least two possibilities: Brother Paphnutius of the Papal Tiara, and Brother Theopompus of the Silver Trumpets. Even if Francis II has taken lately to wearing a psychedelic skull cap with a solar-powered rotor blade on top, the potent symbol of the tiara has never evaporated from the minds of the faithful, and someday, surely, it will come back, when the Lord gives us a Benedict XVII, someone who cares enough about his sacred office to speak and dress accordingly. So the one name goes really well with that hope.

Father Subprior: On the other hand, the silver trumpets that used to fill the air around St Peter's as late as the reign of John XXIII are a poignant remembrance of the glory that was, for the return of which we beg the Lord.

Father Prior: Still, my gut is to go with the Papal Tiara for Ipps.

Father Subprior: Now we come, I think, to the hardest cases: Pablo and Günther.

Father Prior: Do you think it would be unkind to let the name bespeak the truth? For in that case, I think I would give Pablo the name Brother Modestus of the Uncertain Psalmtone, since, try as we may, he cannot master the psalter, and yet loves to belt it out nonetheless!

Father Subprior: No, you should definitely use that name. It would bring humility, which, I'm afraid to say, he needs, as his opinions are a bit immodest. I still shudder a bit when I think of that recreation where he was holding forth at great length about the relative merits of the *ti* versus the *te* in the old Solesmes books. An outsider would have thought he was gnawing on something *serious*, like the pope's Year of Mindless Tolerance for Diversity. Almost nobody knew what Pablo was talking about. It was almost as bad as reading the Heptateuch before bedtime.

Father Prior: Fair enough. I think you've made your point.

Father Subprior: Moving on to Günther… You know what he is like.

Father Prior: He is a dedicated altar server, one of our best and most precise, conversant with Fortescue, O'Connell, Quoëx, and all the other experts; but he can get carried away at times with sacramentals. Not that I'm blaming him in the least; I think it was his deprived childhood, when he was forced to attend tortuously verbose Novus Ordo Masses utterly lacking in sacred symbols, that gave him that almost bloodthirsty taste for holy water and incense. You can almost hear his pulse quickening when we bring up the topic of processions at chapter meetings.

A Day in the Life of a Monastery, Some Years in the Future

Father Subprior: So, let me guess… You are drawn towards Brother Nicephorus of the Perilous Aspergilium or Brother Hilarius of the Pendulous Thurible. Am I right?

Father Prior: You know me so very well, it's disconcerting. Those are exactly the names I had in mind for Günth. And he's got a great sense of humor, so he won't take it amiss.

Father Subprior: Humor is the eighth gift of the Holy Spirit, they say.

Father Prior: Without it, where would we be? Francis II has nearly compelled us to develop an entirely new "sensibility"—a sort of dire seriousness about matters of faith coupled with a frolicsome detachment from all earthly things, including church politics, which has to be the most painfully earthly of all earthly things.

Father Subprior: Sadly true. I used to think it was a waste of time studying Machiavelli and Nietzsche in college. Much later, when I was compelled to move in ecclesiastical circles, it all became clear to me.

Father Prior: Let's get back to our fine young candidates. We were talking earlier about Jean Pierre. I have to wonder if a different name wouldn't suit him better. You recall his heartfelt devotion to Pio Nono. How about Brother Pius of Immemorial Custom?

Father Subprior: Ah yes, the pope of the Syllabus of Errors. Perfect!

Father Prior: Jean Pierre concurs, if anyone does, that the Roman Pontiff cannot and should not "reconcile and harmonize himself with progress, liberalism, and modern civilization"—those immortal closing words of the Syllabus.

Father Subprior: In fact, I will never forget the time I saw him decorating his cell and asked him: "What are all those sheets of paper you've got taped up there by your desk?" His response: "The collected anathemas of the Roman Church. It's comforting to see where the boundaries are—like having streets and sidewalks, paved and mapped. You are more free to move around."

Father Prior: Don't you think it's splendid when candidates practically *force* you to give them certain names? They are too docile to insist, but their gifts make easier work for us. I've always thought the name should fit the person, and be a vibrant sign of the contribution he will make to the Mystical Body.

Father Subprior: I could not possibly disagree. After all, was it not by a singular providence that you, upon your clothing so many years ago, were given the name Brother Hermes of the Allegorical Mass Commentaries?

Father Prior: Just as providential as when you were named Brother Gervase of the Courtly Accretions! I mean, seriously, you can't make up stuff like this. Truth is always stranger than fiction, and reality has its store of surprises for us.

Father Subprior: Wait a minute, that almost sounds like the "God of surprises" that the first Pope Francis used to go on about.

Father Prior: But it's true: He *is* a God of surprises. No one expected the last pope to run off with the neo-Marxist tango-dance juggling troupe *¡Hagan Lío!* that performed in the Paul VI audience hall, and never return, leaving all the curial officials rejoicing. Nothing like that had ever happened before. Usually the popes died in office, from natural causes like overwork, news of foreign invasions, reports from dicasteries, or poison. The fact that he stacked the bench and seemingly rigged the election of Francis II is regrettable, but what can we do about it? There is no rule of law anymore, in the Church or in the world.

Father Subprior: We can always pray for a miracle.

Father Prior: That is exactly it. There are some messes from which only God can deliver us. That is where we are at today. *Libera nos, Domine!* Meanwhile, we cannot waste our time on the latest deviltry from Rome. There is real work to be done: the *Opus Dei*, the building of our monastery, and the building of our souls. All this is work enough. May the Lord bless this labor and grant us a miracle besides.

Father Subprior: I just heard the bell for Vespers—Günth sure gives that rope a manly tug! Or should I now say, Brother Nicephorus of the Perilous Aspergilium?

Father Prior: Perhaps, after all, Brother Hilarius of the Pendulous Thurible. Thank you, Brother Gervase, for your considerable help. I simply could not complete such tasks without your counsel.

Father Subprior: Blessed be God! Now let's be off.

17

"It's Time We Stopped the Musical Starvation Diet"

An Interview with Diane Montagna

Dr Kwasniewski, can you tell me something about your background in church music?

I've been composing for about 25 years, mostly sacred choral music but also instrumental works and a few secular works. My first serious lessons in composition and conducting took placed with a wonderful teacher, Roy Horton, who was organist at Delbarton School in Morristown, New Jersey. I fell in love with music and threw myself into it more than I had done with any other subject up until that point.

When I arrived at Thomas Aquinas College [in California], I had the good fortune to be asked by the main choir director, who lived quite a distance from the college, to be the assistant choir director. I started leading choir practices and even leading the choir at Mass on Sundays. It was a total immersion experience, like being thrown into the deep end of the pool without knowing how to swim very well. The four years in college of working intensively with the choir really fired my imagination.

Can you be more specific about what it was that fired your imagination?

What was appealing to me was the Gregorian chant and the polyphony. In college I was in the schola for four years and sang the proper chants of the Mass, Sunday after Sunday. We also sang polyphonic Mass ordinaries and motets. That was my first serious acquaintance with sacred music: singing Palestrina, Victoria, Byrd, the great Renaissance composers. I suppose you could say I had the best models to work with and I tried to imitate them in my own compositions, although these were clumsy at first. With trial and error, through study and hard work, I got to a point sometime after graduation where I was writing music that choirs wanted to sing and that I felt confident putting forward to the public.

Someone could raise the objection: why don't we just sing chant and Palestrina? The composers of this music, whether anonymous or named, are clearly geniuses and we can't equal their work, so why bother?

There's nothing wrong, of course, with continually going back to the classics of the past; the Second Vatican Council says we should do that.[1] But every generation should have something beautiful that it can add to the treasury, because every generation wants to make an offering to God. That's why the Council says that Catholic composers, inspired by the past, should make their own contribution to the store of the arts.[2]

Another way to look at it is that modern works of art can (and should) have a certain modern feel to them, so that they seem to emerge from and speak to our age. For instance, contemporary composers make use of harmonies that are more adventurous, that go beyond the rules of earlier centuries—think of the music of Arvo Pärt, Morten Lauridsen, Frank La Rocca, Kevin Allen. Their music is beautiful *and* distinctively modern.

Isn't there a danger, though, with modern music—that it can alienate listeners? Maybe by being too dissonant?

Yes, for sure, we have struggled with that problem, although the atonal revolution of the twentieth century has mostly died out by

1. See *Sacrosanctum Concilium*, n. 112 and n. 144.
2. Ibid., n. 121.

now, and the "new tonality" has taken its place. Any church composer worth his salt understands that one has to have a certain "conservatism" when writing sacred music. Whatever is "modern" in the piece should not overshadow the whole character of it so that it seems *only* modern and cut off from the past. The past offers us perennially valid models.

If you look at the great composers and sculptors and architects of our Western civilization—the ones who produced works that countless people still marvel over—they did the same thing. None of them ever tried to start from scratch. They were always building off of the models that came before. That's part of the humility of a great artist. It's standing on the shoulders of giants. If you're a composer, you try to learn from the great composers; you don't ignore them and think you can do better than they have done. I find it extremely energizing, this constant dialogue between past and present, between masterpieces that set the bar high and our own efforts to enrich the repertoire.

In any case, sacred music is alive and well. It has been shown again and again that worthwhile new things can come from age-old ideals. It is a privilege to be able to serve Our Lord and His Church in this way.

What motivates you to write a particular piece of sacred music?

Often there is a particular liturgical need for a piece, perhaps a simpler setting because it will be quicker or easier to learn with amateur choristers—and when you're singing week after week and don't have a lot of rehearsal time, that can be very helpful.

Receiving a commission to write a motet or a Mass is highly motivating, because then you know that someone desires *your* work in particular, which is encouraging. They are looking for a special, custom-made work of art, rather than relying on free online downloads of amateur editions of long-dead composers. The commission usually concerns a special occasion and offers a particular text to work with. All these things give a focus and an impetus to the work.

Can you say something about the creative process?

Creativity is not something that's on tap like beer. If you produce something like that, it will be pedestrian and uninspired, more like an exercise or a homework assignment. A piece of music that is going to touch people is something that's a gift. And you just have to keep putting yourself in the way of that gift. I think it's like the Christian life in general. You work as hard as you can to dispose yourself to God's grace, but in the end you know that it's going to be a gift from Him, and you can't claim it or demand it.

Practically speaking, I need a block of free time, a quiet house, a piano, a music notebook, and a good pencil with a good eraser. I like to scribble down ideas, motifs, chords. Often it will take a few years to finish a piece. The draft sits around for a while before I see the overall direction it needs, or the finishing touches. In a few happy cases, a strong idea turns into a complete piece in a day or two.

You are working within a tradition that goes back centuries. But while one can find Church legislation on music from every century, people tend to see Pope St Pius X as the one who inaugurated the modern Magisterium on the subject. Why was he, specifically, the one who paid so much attention to it?

When he was a bishop, Giuseppe Sarto, the future Pope Pius X, heard a lot of crummy music in church. In the late nineteenth century, the problem wasn't the sacro-pop or pseudo-folk music we have today; it was the rage for Italian romantic opera, a sentimental, theatrical, emotional genre—very distracting for worship. Sarto recognized its ecclesiastical adaptations as second-rate entertainment music rather than first-rate sacred music. So one of the first things he did when he ascended the papal throne in 1903 was to issue the motu proprio *Tra le sollecitudini* on the restoration of authentic sacred music.

This document reflects Pius X's deep love of the Church's liturgy and his ardent desire, as a pastor, to restore it to the full splendor, nobility, and sacredness that should belong to its celebration. He knew that the first and most important place to begin was with the music. He demanded that everyone return to the purity and simplicity and beauty of Gregorian chant. While his appeal didn't meet with acceptance everywhere, it did create a movement in favor of Gregorian chant, including all sorts of programs for schoolchildren around the world. As a result, chant was employed much more between 1903 and the Second Vatican Council, and generally with a better sound, than had been the case for a couple of centuries prior.

Did Pope Pius X's successors deliver the same message?

Yes, absolutely. After Pius X, Pius XI in 1928 issued an important document called *Divini Cultus* where he repeated the same principles and urged the Christian people to *sing* the chants that belong to them, especially the Ordinary of the Mass. Then you have Pius XII who wrote several times about sacred music, for example, in the encyclicals *Mediator Dei* (1947) and *Musicae Sacrae* (1955). So we have much from Pius XII that enunciates the same teaching. John Paul II, who had such a long pontificate, touched on music many times. I published an article that summarizes his teaching.[3] Probably his main contribution was the chirograph on the centenary of *Tra le Sollecitudini* in 2003. Finally, Benedict XVI is the pope who, of all popes in history, has the most detailed and the most profound teaching about Church music—one thinks of texts like the post-synodal apostolic exhortation *Sacramentum Caritatis* of 2007, his books *The Spirit of the Liturgy* and *A New Song for the Lord,* and so much else. All of these are immensely worth our time, since they do so much more than declaim rules or traditions; they offer a thorough explanation of the rationale behind the Church's teaching.

Can you give us that rationale, in a nutshell?

The root principles are given in St Pius X's motu proprio. Sacred music should be *holy*—that is, it should be characterized by a kind of recognizable and palpable holiness. You should be able to hear it and say "This is music for the temple of God; this is not profane or

3. "John Paul II on Sacred Music," *Sacred Music,* vol. 133, n. 2 (Summer 2006): 4–22. This article may be downloaded at http://www.musicasacra.com/publications/sacredmusic/pdf/sm133-2.pdf.

secular music." This is not music from the cinema or from Broadway or from the disco or the campfire, but it's music for the temple of God. Then, the music should be *good*; it should be artistically well-crafted and noble. Nothing of poor quality, nothing shoddy, nothing that's trite or banal. The third quality he talks about is that it should be *universal*. It should be such as to characterize the Catholic Church, which is the same all throughout the world, celebrating the same mysteries with fixed liturgical rites. So, in other words, it shouldn't be the music of a particular tribe or camp or school or subculture. It should be as universal as possible.

Pope Pius X says Gregorian chant is perfectly these three things: it's holy, it's artistically beautiful, and it's universal. This is why it's the normative music, the exemplar, the gold standard. Therefore, the pope concludes that other music is welcome into the temple *to the extent that* it embodies these qualities of chant. Renaissance polyphony receives special praise because it derives its melodic vocabulary and liturgical spirit from the chant.

Don't people say that Vatican II got rid of this whole view of things?

It's incredible how much nonsense people attribute to "Vatican II." In *Sacrosanctum Concilium*, the Council Fathers reiterated this teaching of St Pius X and went on to say something no pope or ecumenical council had ever said before—namely, that because Gregorian chant is the music proper to the Roman rite, it should have the chief place (or as some translations say, "pride of place") in the liturgy. No qualifications were made: in *each and every* liturgy. Chant should always have chief place because it's the very music *of* the rite. It's not just music tacked on to the rite, it's the music that grew up with it, "bone of its bone and flesh of its flesh." Gregorian chant *is* the Roman rite in its musical vesture.

That certainly doesn't sound like the view that has prevailed in the past fifty years.

The Council's teaching on the primacy of Gregorian chant was ignored or belittled because of the modernist spirit behind the liturgical reform and its implementation. Still, the teaching is *there*, giving expression to a fundamental reality of Catholic tradition, and anyone who wants to be Roman Catholic can follow it.

The first thing we have to recognize is that the Church's teaching about sacred music is *true*. It's not just a subjective opinion, something culturally relative, that we can take or leave. There really *are* objective qualities that belong to properly liturgical music, and the Church has repeatedly named what those qualities are. Whether we take up old music or write and sing new music, we need to follow those principles. This is how church music thrives and how it serves the true spiritual needs of the faithful.

Some people say that the Church's teaching on sacred music is no longer relevant to our modern, pluralistic situation. How would you respond?

It seems to me that our contemporary situation is *more*, not less, in need of the Church's wise counsels and rich tradition.

Human beings need beautiful things; human beings long for beautiful music that is suited to divine worship. The liturgy is supposed to be special; it's not supposed to seem like an everyday affair, or look and sound like the prevailing popular culture. It should be different, distinctive, an encounter with the transcendent God. When Catholics encounter this mystery through music—and also, of course, through other things: vestments, architecture, the *ars celebrandi*, the way the priest and the ministers bear themselves at the altar—it actually helps them to know their faith better. This isn't some abstract aesthetic preference. It's about recognizing the distinctiveness of the Catholic Faith and living it more fully. The music we use at Mass is not just window dressing; it's essential to who we are and what we're doing.

Why has there been a hundred years of papal teaching on this subject? If it was just a small matter, it wouldn't have been on the agenda for such a long time and gotten into the Council. People who want to be faithful to the magisterial documents and who want to bring out the treasures of the Christian tradition know what to do. The path is clear for those who have the right understanding of what the liturgy is, and, sadly, the path is not clear for those who don't.

You say the liturgy is "not supposed to look or sound like popular culture." Why is this?

I learned this crucial point from Benedict XVI, who is concerned about the deplorable state of Church music in most places. He recognizes it as an invasion of secularism, a sort of pathetic attempt on the part of the Church to compete with secular culture. Somebody once said about Christian rock music that "it's only relevant for five minutes, and four of those minutes were not worth it." Or as another person said: "If you can't deliver a product that's ten times better than your competitor, you shouldn't even bother." And the Church can't do that with secular culture. She's not meant to do that, and she'll never succeed.

What's necessary is to bend the stick in the opposite direction and make sure that the liturgy is holy, sacred, reverent in every way. Music plays a huge role in that necessary orientation to God. In fact, music is the most obvious element of the liturgy, even if it's not the most important. It's the thing that hits you most, affects you most immediately. If it's wrong, the whole experience is wrong, and the meaning of the event will be compromised, too—maybe even corrupted. But when it's right, it gives glory to God and assists in the sanctification of the faithful. What a noble ministry, what an immense responsibility!

There is a practical difficulty, isn't there? People in parishes where the Ordinary Form (Novus Ordo) is celebrated can be intimidated by what they perceive as the difficulty of singing chant or polyphony.

I'll admit it can be a little intimidating at first. Modern Western culture is really not a singing culture and is certainly not a high culture anymore; we've become simplistic in our tastes and limited in our abilities. The realm of sacred music seems remote, esoteric, difficult. And we shouldn't kid ourselves: it *does* require discipline and hard work; anything great does. Man is made for this greatness, and God deserves it. On the other hand, it's not as hard as some people might think, especially if one sets realistic goals.

For fifty years we have been not only underestimating the potential of Catholics to learn better music but positively insulting their intelligence with second-rate ditties. I know of people who have actually been driven away from the Catholic Church because of the horrible music! In this way we have deprived ourselves of giving and receiving blessings from one another in the form of music. It's time that we stopped the musical starvation diet and reached for richer fare.

Can you give examples of "realistic goals" to get us to "richer fare"?

Singing the Ordinary of the Mass is quite an achievable goal and the people in the pews will pick it up, too, since chant is pleasant to sing, and the melodies are more natural and less demanding in range and rhythm than the vocal gymnastics of a lot of today's church songs. I've been to Mass in many places around the world where congregations are accustomed to singing the Ordinary of the Mass with a surprising amount of gusto. It is *our Catholic music*, and we can and should be proud of it!

Let's say you wish to incorporate chant into the Mass. Chants are always sung in unison, so you don't have to worry about splitting into parts. Those who can sing a hymn melody can learn to sing a Kyrie, Gloria, Sanctus, or Agnus Dei, or a Marian antiphon like the Salve Regina or Alma Redemptoris Mater. You get together and you start with simpler chants, and you build from there.

By the way, none of this has to be accompanied by an organ; I have always found it easier to sing chant *without* organ because you don't have to try to coordinate with a musician and you end up using your own ears better. There is nothing so uplifting and so refreshingly *human* as the sound of a church full of people chanting in unison, with no amplification and no instruments.

The Propers of the Mass—the Introit, Gradual, Alleluia, Offertory, and Communion antiphons—are more challenging. They were written by and for trained cantors who know their stuff. There are, nevertheless, simplified settings of the Propers that one can look into for getting started.

How about polyphony?

Unlike chant, polyphony requires a group of individuals who are musically talented enough to be able to sing their own parts, in good pitch and correct timing, along with others who are singing different parts at the same time. This presupposes at least one competently trained musician who is familiar with the appropriate repertoire and its stylistic demands and who can confidently lead the singers. Even so, communities of any decent size will have the "raw material," if only someone can lure out the singers and get them to rehearse.

You haven't mentioned the organ yet. What about its role?

The teaching of the Catholic Church is clear: the organ is the primary and most fitting instrument for sacred music in the church, period, end of discussion. This has been taught so many times that it cannot be disputed, and the experience of great organ music is the closest thing I know to a totally unanswerable argument of fact. Just as chant and polyphony should be present in every parish and every school, so too should organ music resound in every church and chapel. We need a new generation of organists, well-formed musically and well-informed theologically, who can add once again the glory of this king of the instruments to our worship.

Still, as glorious as it is, the organ is not simply indispensable to a sacred music program, at least in its initial phase. With one organizer, a few good voices, and adequate pastoral support, sacred music can blossom anywhere.

For young people who are serious about sacred music and what they can contribute, what would you recommend?

The irreplaceable foundation is to become intimately acquainted with authentic sacred music. Although you can do this by listening to excellent recordings, it is better to get involved with a parish or a religious community that is serious about having this music. You can be a member of the congregation and soak it in, or a member of the choir so that you sing the music and get to know it firsthand, whether it's chant or polyphony or traditional hymnody.

The next big step is to attend a workshop of the Church Music Association of America where you will have an "immersion experience" of singing the Church's great music, learning from teachers who really know how to teach it. The CMAA has an annual Sacred Music Colloquium and multiple chant workshops throughout the year that can be life-changing and unforgettable experiences. Meeting and working with many other musicians who are attracted to the same beautiful music is a sovereign antidote to the despondency of feeling "all alone" at times.

Speaking more broadly, it's a good idea to visit blogs like *New Liturgical Movement* and *OnePeterFive* in order to keep learning about Catholic culture and the liturgy. We need inspiration and consolation, encouragement and concrete ideas, as we seek to restore the sacred in our own little corner of the world.

In your view, are there reasons for hope, in spite of the postconciliar chaos?

Recent years have witnessed the reintroduction of sacred music in quite a number of parishes and chapels throughout the world, thanks in large measure to the stirring example and writings of Benedict XVI. In my experience as a teacher, young people have a hunger for traditional Catholicism and are excited when they discover sacred music. The religious orders that are flourishing are, in most cases, ones that have maintained or reintroduced Gregorian chant. Yes, we are living in a difficult and chaotic period, but you can see shoots of green pushing up here and there through the gray volcanic rubble. It's enough to presage the regrowth of a lush forest. Our Lord never abandons His Church. He patiently calls us back to the "beauty of holiness" when we have forsaken it.

Could we turn our attention to a more particular topic? I'm thinking of the problem of choirs. It seems that the only way to implement all the good things we've been talking about is to have robust, well-trained choirs in every parish or chapel. But that's hardly what one finds

*around the world. As a matter of fact, choirs were discouraged and dis-
banded after the Council, on the grounds that the music was now
going to be "of the people, by the people, for the people." And where
choirs do exist, the music they sing is generally so bad that many people would prefer them to go away for good. So a crucial element is
recovering a clear sense of the nature, purpose, and necessity of choirs.*

*We could start with their history. What do we know about the ori-
gins of choirs in the Catholic Church?*

In the Old Testament, especially in Chronicles and in the subtitles
to the Psalms, we see that the ancient Hebrews deployed teams of
singers and musicians to chant their liturgies. This custom continued in the early Church, indebted as it was to Jewish precedents and
influenced by the strong connection found in all religions (including those of Greece and Rome) between cultic activity and ceremonial music. The early Christians tended towards sobriety and
simplicity in their chanting: they were attracted to the primacy of
the Word, the *Logos*, and wanted to put behind them the carnal
indulgence characteristic of much of the ancient world's popular
religiosity. From what we can tell, Christian music of antiquity was
a relatively unadorned chanting of sacred texts. A close comparison
might be the antiphons and psalm tones of the Divine Office.

But when did choirs as such come into being?

No matter how enthusiastic the baptized are, musical talents will
never be evenly distributed among the members of the body—nor
should we expect them to be, if we think of St Paul's teaching about
the variety of gifts given by the Spirit. There will always be, for example, the cantor who can sing more easily, beautifully, and edifyingly.

As the Church's liturgy developed in the post-Constantinian
period, the chants of worship became more important, elaborate,
and numerous. They became a genuine artistic *corpus* demanding
skill of execution. Thus were born the first *scholae cantorum* or
chant choirs. While more familiar and repeated chants, such as the
Mass Ordinary and the congregational responses, would have been
sung by all present, as they are today at parishes in touch with the

Church's musical heritage, the *scholae* came into being for the mel-ismatic (melodiously complex and extended) chants. For the first millennium, of course, we are speaking only of monophonic or single-part music. Polyphony did not emerge until the second millennium, and with its birth, the choir, in the familiar sense of the word, was born.

Say more about the development of polyphony in the Church.

Prior to early experiments in organum or harmonized chant, the music you would have heard in church was monophonic chant, that is, music of a single unanimous melody. It is comparatively easy to sing chant with a large group and still stay together, as when Catholics today sing a plainchant Gloria or Credo. But once those enterprising medieval composers began working with multiple simultaneous parts, you had a surprisingly quick development of music *for experts*, that is, skillful singers who could tune to each other, keep exact time, and do all that a successful performance requires.

Over a few centuries this acorn grew into the majestic oak tree that we call Renaissance polyphony—from the School of Notre Dame to Machaut, Ockeghem to Du Fay, Josquin to Palestrina, Victoria to Byrd. The resulting body of work, comprising thousands upon thousands of Masses, motets, and other choral works, is unlike anything the world had ever known before or has ever known since. It is music of spiritual peace and sensuous beauty, prayerful intensity, spacious thought, purified emotions, lofty aspirations, modesty and naturalness. It flows along with the gentle rhythmic pulse of chant, it sparkles with the suppleness of the medieval modes.

As music of the highest artistic excellence, inspired by centuries of Catholic faith and nurtured in an age of liturgy in its full splendor, Renaissance polyphony is second only to chant itself in its perfect suitability for the public, formal, solemn worship of God. It is music wholly in service of the sacred text and of the sacred liturgy. It is sanctified and sanctifying music.

How did this development affect the role of the choir in the liturgy?

Polyphony is demanding. You need singers who are well trained and who really understand the character of the music. So it is not music for everyone to sing, but music for some to sing, while everyone else has the privilege of listening to it as part of a collective act of worship in which each plays his or her own part.

So the choir obviously became very important. Did this marginalize the people, as some say?

It depends a great deal on the century you are looking at, as well as the geographical area. From what I have read, it seems that popular liturgical chanting was found in many places and times throughout Church history—but choirs did occasionally eclipse that involvement, turning the liturgy into something more like a concert performance.

The popes from St Pius X onwards, concerned about the replacement of congregational chanting with (often second-rate) concert performances, urged the faithful to be instructed in chant so that they could sing the parts of the Mass that pertain to them. For its part, Vatican II's Constitution on the Sacred Liturgy, *Sacrosanctum Concilium*, stated explicitly: "Steps should be taken so that the faithful may also be able to say or to sing together in Latin those parts of the Ordinary of the Mass which pertain to them" (n. 54).

The healthy instinct of the Church has always been for a wise balance between liturgical singing in which everyone can participate and liturgical singing that is rightly entrusted to choirs or scholas. As John Paul II and Benedict XVI taught, choirs dedicated to this more exalted repertoire perform a genuine service for the faithful themselves, by lifting their minds to the sublime beauty of God and prompting interior acts of praise, blessing, adoration, glorification, contrition, and thanksgiving.

Your mention of Vatican II makes me want to raise a common objection. Many today will say that trained choirs no longer have a role, because all the liturgical music should be sung by all the people. Was this the Council's teaching?

This is one of the greatest and most damaging fallacies promoted after the Council, by people who should have known better. The Council's Constitution on the Sacred Liturgy gives a nuanced teaching that includes *both* an emphasis on congregational participation *and* the indispensable role of trained choirs—the familiar "both/and" of Catholicism. How can we forget such a statement as this: "The musical tradition of the universal Church is a treasure of inestimable value, greater even than that of *any other art.*"[4] Astonishing, when you think of all the cathedrals, basilicas, statues, monuments, vestments, vessels, windows, paintings, poetry, and prose of Christendom. Sacred music tops them all, because it is an integral part of the solemn liturgy, intimately bound up with its very words, and "adds delight to prayer, fosters unity of minds, and confers greater solemnity upon the sacred rites."[5] The conciliar Fathers tell us quite specifically: "The treasure of sacred music is to be preserved and fostered with great care."[6] You can't do this by chucking it out the window, ignoring it, or downgrading it!

The Constitution continues: "Choirs must be diligently promoted," as long as they do not take away from the people the participation that is due to them. This means that the people sing what belongs to their role—not that they sing everything. The Council never says that the people should sing everything, and they could never have said it without doing violence to the entire history of liturgy over the past 3,000 years. The liturgy involves many roles, many elements, many levels of music, and all should have their due place.

Finally, not content with generalities, the conciliar Fathers single out chant and polyphony for special praise: "The Church acknowledges Gregorian chant as specially suited to the Roman liturgy: therefore, other things being equal, it should be given chief place in liturgical services."[7] This "other things being equal," *ceteris paribus*, means that *even if* other types of music are taken as equal, Grego-

---

4. *Sacrosanctum Concilium*, n. 112, emphasis added.
5. Ibid.
6. Ibid., n. 114.
7. Ibid., n. 116.

rian chant should *still* enjoy the "chief place" (this is closer to the Latin original than "pride of place") *because* it is the chant specially suited to the Roman liturgy, the one that grew up with it from its infancy and was always the musical vesture of its texts.

Then the document concludes: "But other kinds of sacred music, especially polyphony, are by no means excluded from liturgical celebrations [by chant's pride of place], so long as they accord with the spirit of the liturgical action." Note: *especially* polyphony. Could anything have been clearer? Alas, it was not for want of clarity that sacred music was destroyed, but because of ideological commitments to a supposititious "People's Liturgy" that had no real existence in Church history and could have no real existence in theology.

You have made it clear that the Council is favorable to traditional sacred music and to the contribution made by choirs. Do recent popes endorse this teaching, too?

In one of the most important addresses on the liturgy he ever gave—the *ad limina* address to the bishops of the Northwestern United States on October 9, 1998—Pope John Paul II went to enormous lengths to correct a one-sided view of active participation that was (and still is) far too prevalent:

> The sharing of all the baptized in the one priesthood of Jesus Christ is the key to understanding the Council's call for "full, conscious and active participation" in the liturgy. Full participation certainly means that every member of the community has a part to play in the liturgy; and in this respect a great deal has been achieved in parishes and communities across your land. But full participation does *not* mean that everyone does everything, since this would lead to a clericalizing of the laity and a laicizing of the priesthood; and this was not what the Council had in mind. The liturgy, like the Church, is intended to be hierarchical and polyphonic, respecting the different roles assigned by Christ and allowing all the different voices to blend in one great hymn of praise. Active participation certainly means that, in gesture, word, song and service, all the members of the community take part in an act of worship, which is anything but inert or passive. Yet active

participation does not preclude the active passivity of silence, stillness and listening: indeed, it demands it. Worshippers are not passive, for instance, when listening to the readings or the homily, or following the prayers of the celebrant, and the chants and music of the liturgy. These are experiences of silence and stillness, but they are in their own way profoundly active. In a culture which neither favors nor fosters meditative quiet, the art of interior listening is learned only with difficulty. Here we see how the liturgy, though it must always be properly inculturated, must also be countercultural.

John Paul II speaks here of how important it is for the faithful to learn the art of "active listening." Here is where some soul-searching is necessary. How often do we let the words of the liturgy float right over our heads, while our minds are a thousand miles away? How often do we *say* the words of the liturgy without even being conscious we have said them? The vernacularization of the Mass contributed significantly to this problem, since it fostered the illusion that as long as something is in your native language, you'll pay attention to it and make it your own. Not only is this not necessarily true, but experience has often shown the opposite. The vernacular is our comfort zone, where we can take much for granted, where "half-listening" is terribly easy. On the other hand, when people encounter *Latin* in the liturgy, this strange and hieratic language often compels them to sit up and pay attention, to wonder what is being said and why. The very language proclaims that we are engaged in an act that is not an ordinary affair, that we are entering a time and space set aside, consecrated to God alone.

But to get back to John Paul II's point: the faithful are to *internalize* the chants and music of the liturgy, so that the message they carry, particularly through the beauty of the melodies and harmonies, becomes the seed of meditation and contemplation, drawing us more intimately into the mystery of God.

I would go further and argue that we are more in need of the earnest beauty of traditional sacred music today than ever. Great sacred music—especially from past centuries—can help us break free of the narrow and artificial confines of modernity, to catch a glimpse of the wonder of God, the enchanted cosmos, and the promise of a new heaven and a new earth. It is a potent aid to reverence, devotion, recollection, and self-transcendence.

Benedict XVI is a fierce critic of what he calls "utility music," saying that its banality is unworthy of the Christian liturgy. How does this fit in with what you are saying about choirs?

Pope Benedict says somewhere that it is not enough to have music that "works," that supplies a certain function, in the manner of a commercial ditty; it has to be better than that. It needs to be suitable for God by being *worthy* of Him, as much as we can make it. The Church's tradition is positively overflowing with such worthy offerings. One could spend ten or twenty lifetimes singing the great music of the Catholic Church and never get to the end of the repertoire.

So, although we can and should add to this treasury—otherwise I myself would not be a composer of church music!—we would be fools if we did not continue to value what we have inherited from the past. Who but a fool would say that gold from yesterday is worth less than gold from today, or that a diamond a thousand years old is no longer up-to-date and relevant? Beautiful things are never outdated; they are always valid, always suitable, always worthy, always new.

In 2012, Pope Benedict addressed some inspiring words to members of *scholae cantorum* from across Italy. His whole address is worth reading. He asks why the Council teaches that music is a "necessary and integral" part of the liturgy, and answers:

> Certainly not for purely aesthetic reasons, in a superficial sense, but because it cooperates, precisely through its beauty, in nourishing and expressing the faith, and so [redounds] to the glory of God and the sanctification of the faithful, which are the ends of sacred music. For this reason I wish to thank you for the precious service that you render: the music that you perform is not an accessory or only an external ornament of the liturgy, but *it is liturgy itself.* You help the whole assembly to praise God, to make his Word enter into the depths of the heart: with song you pray and help others pray, and you participate in the song and prayer of the liturgy that embraces the whole of creation in glorifying the Creator.

What a pep talk for any and every church choir!

Then, recalling how the famous poet Paul Claudel was converted by the beauty of the Christmas liturgy at Notre Dame, Pope Benedict continues:

> We need not have recourse to illustrious persons to think of how many people have been touched in the depths of their soul listening to sacred music, and of how many more have felt themselves, like Claudel, newly drawn to God by the beauty of liturgical music. And here, dear friends, you have an important role: work to improve the quality of liturgical song without being afraid to recover and value the great musical tradition of the Church, which has in Gregorian chant and polyphony two of its highest expressions, as Vatican II itself states (*SC* 116). And I would like to stress that the active participation of the whole people of God in the liturgy does *not* consist only in speaking, but also in listening, in welcoming the Word with the senses and the spirit; and this holds also for sacred music. You, who have the gift of song, can make the heart of many people sing in liturgical celebrations.

Here we see how John Paul II and Benedict XVI were of one mind in their understanding of the teaching of Vatican II.

So the critics of choirs and of their polyphonic music are not being faithful to the Magisterium?

Let's put it this way: if there is opposition to a regular and judicious use of the great polyphonic sacred music of our heritage, or if there is opposition to choirs singing while the faithful listen, then obviously we are looking at unfaithfulness to Vatican II and to all of the popes from St Pius X to Benedict XVI.

On the other hand, let's be fair: there can be "choral abuses." For example, if the choir is not sufficiently well-trained and capable of handling the repertoire, it will not edify the hearers or give glory to God. If they are *always* singing everything and the people in the pews *never* sing anything—not even the Kyrie or the Credo or "Et cum spiritu tuo"—then the choir is taking over like a bully. If the choir's choice of music is too eccentric or tilts too much to the modern, let's say all twentieth-century French impressionistic music, they will not be following the teaching of the Church. On most occasions, the predominant music ought to be Gregorian chant; the people should be singing what belongs to them, too; and the choir will be providing polyphonic motets either from the Renaissance or in a style inspired by and compatible with liturgical chant.

So you think it is always wrong for the choir to do all the music and for the congregation to sing nothing? And, while we're at it, what about orchestral Masses?

On solemn or special occasions, it can be perfectly fine for the choir to take a much larger role, doing a polyphonic Mass Ordinary and polyphonic Mass Propers, or even music with orchestral accompaniment. But this should not be the norm, because it would not be compatible with the best traditions of the Church, the theology of the liturgy as a communal hierarchical action, and the oft-repeated teaching of the Magisterium.

Catholics have always had a strong sense that the liturgical calendar features intense times and relaxed times, if I can put it that way. At the intense times—above all from Christmas to Epiphany, and the weeks from Palm Sunday to Low Sunday, and around Pentecost—the level of music ought to be much higher, much fuller, and the role of the choir increases accordingly. At more relaxed times, let's say the many "green Sundays" after Pentecost, the choir is still important, but the people should also have their part in the singing of the liturgy. It is all about "both/and," not "either/or."

We've touched on this in various ways, but I'd like to ask you if you have any further thoughts on the problem of the choir as an "endangered species" today, and the poor quality of music in general. How did we get here and how do we go forward?

The omnipresent false understanding of "active participation" led almost overnight to the marginalization of chant and polyphony and a dismantling of choirs and scholas. This was happening at the very time that the Vatican was saying the opposite. For instance, the Sacred Congregation of Rites, issuing norms about sacred music in the wake of *Sacrosanctum Concilium* in a document called *Musicam Sacram* (1967), stated: "Because of the liturgical ministry it performs, the choir—or the *capella musica*, or *schola cantorum*—deserves particular mention. Its role has become something *of yet greater importance and weight* by reason of the norms of the Council concerning the liturgical renewal." Amazing, isn't it?

There's more: "Its duty is, in effect, to ensure the proper performance of the parts which belong to it, according to the different kinds of music sung, and to encourage the active participation of the faithful in the singing." The document recognizes the different types of music and different roles. Then it draws the practical conclusion: "Therefore: (a) There should be choirs, or *capellae*, or *scholae cantorum*, especially in cathedrals and other major churches, in seminaries and religious houses of studies, and they should be carefully encouraged. (b) It would also be desirable for similar choirs to be set up in smaller churches." Our marching orders haven't changed since then: we need to set up choirs everywhere, to perform the distinctive and important role that belongs to them in the sacred liturgy, and to foster a higher standard of artistic beauty and congregational singing.

For choirs to succeed, knowledge is necessary—knowledge of the Roman liturgy and its spirituality, structure, and requirements, of the relevant legislation, of the musical repertoire itself and how to interpret it, teach it, and inspire in others a commitment to it. This may sound impossibly complicated, but it's not. Resources for learning and leading church music are better and more copious today than they have ever been, and only the leader of the ensemble needs to be fully versed in them, so that he or she can convey to the singers what they need to know, in a process of ongoing musical and liturgical formation. I always recommend that people attend the summertime Sacred Music Colloquium of the Church Music Association of America (CMAA) or some similar event. The practical experience and advice one acquires and the personal connections one makes vastly repay the investment of time and money.

Is it time for a renaissance of children's choirs and good music in parochial schools?

Yes, absolutely! Several children's choirs across the country are doing great work with and for their young people. One of the most incredible choir schools in the country is the Madeleine Choir School in Salt Lake City. Once you hear what those children can do, you will *never* say to yourself again: "This music is too difficult for us today and too remote from our times." On the contrary, it sounds glorious and speaks to us profoundly.

The Ward Method is particularly effective in teaching music and deserves to become the standard feature of Catholic schools that it once was in healthier times. Children are unbelievably quick to absorb the music, to learn the scales, the solfège, the chant, and to memorize repertoire. They put us older folks to shame. They have an enormous capacity and a positive attitude that are, sadly, rarely tapped into. "Let the little children come to me and do not hinder them," said our Lord.[8] Let the children sing His praises and in that way come to Him and bring others to Him.

What do you see as benefits for children and young people being raised singing sacred music?

The benefits are many and deep. There are psychological and physiological benefits to singing and making music. There is the intellectual component: it is a type of learning that expands the mind, puts you in possession of a whole set of skills you would not otherwise have. You are inducted into an immense cultural heritage, something uniquely great in our Western tradition. Above all, there are the spiritual blessings—being conformed to beauty-in-motion, having one's mind and heart imbued with order and harmony, receiving the doctrine and piety of the Catholic faith in a powerfully interior and holistic way. The music becomes a part of us and we find ourselves in the music.

In the first millennium of Christianity, all the sacred music was learned orally; the singers carried it in their heart, while it carried them in their life of prayer. And the liturgy and its music blossomed in thousands of monasteries, from which the faith went forth into

8. Matthew 19:14.

every land and people. That was how the old evangelization succeeded, and that is the way our new evangelization will succeed, too.

As a choir director, do you have any stories of young people being transformed through singing in a choir?

I have seen so many individuals transformed in my 25 years of working with choirs that it would be hard to know where to start! At both my alma mater [Thomas Aquinas College] and Wyoming Catholic College, the students in choir come to love the music they sing so much that they take their stuffed choir binders with them after graduation and look for ways to bring the music to the places they go. A few have contacted me to say that they are now in charge of parish choirs or music classes for children. Some are in monasteries or convents where they spend the day (and often part of the night) singing praises to the Lord, sometimes with the same melodies they sang in college. Other students marry and pass along this priceless treasure to their children. There is a ripple effect.

Do you have any final thoughts on the topic of sacred music?

Most touching to me are the students who say, after their first semester in choir, "I have never had the chance to sing this kind of music before. It is so beautiful, so prayerful, and fits the Mass so well. Why is all this so rare? Why can't everyone enjoy this blessing?"

Indeed, why not? We have a lot of rebuilding to do. This is no time for melancholy regrets and bitter complaints. We need to bring our heritage back into our churches, where it belongs—and where choirs will always have a dignified and irreplaceable ministry to carry out.

18

In the Reign of Pope Leo XIV

Father Remigius: My dear Father Subprior, what a world of difference a new pope makes! I could hardly believe my eyes when I saw the latest issue of *L'Osservatore Romano*.

Brother Willibrord: Well, of course—when Our Lord entrusted the keys of the kingdom to Peter, he knew that it would be "for better and for worse." We suffered long enough under the worse part, and now we are given a relief past all our deserts. I take it you're referring to Pope Leo XIV's establishment of the *Consilium ad Reprehendendam "Formam Ordinariam."*

Father: Yes, and all I can say is, it's about time!

Brother: Did you read about all the subcommittees? Surely you read the fine print...

Father: My favorite was the Subcommittee for the Restoration and Augmentation of Useful Repetitions. I remember, so many years ago, Joseph Ratzinger talking about such things, but the Church was not ready for his wisdom.

Brother: True enough, though it also can't be denied that he threw in the towel in our moment of direst need and took himself out of the picture far too soon. His resignation and its aftermath crippled the movement of restoration and opened the door to years of chaos and suffering.

Father: Still, we owe him a great deal, and we shouldn't let his resignation completely overshadow the good he did and the intelligence he brought to bear on the liturgy.

Brother. Without a doubt. Another thing Benedict XVI longed for was the reconciliation of the Society of St Pius X. Wasn't it a wonder past wonders when, last month, the Society was finally recognized as fully in communion with the Catholic Church and loaded with special dignities and privileges? Its thousands of priests and religious will be a shot in the arm of the Mystical Body, that's for sure!

Father: And what a surprise when the pope in his Bull *Percussit Gladio* not only acknowledged their full communion but lauded their fidelity to the traditional teaching of the Catholic Church and their courage in standing up to the confusions introduced during and after the Second Vatican Council! Who could have imagined that under Francis II?

Brother: The best line from the Bull, I think, was this one: "For too many decades, we have had not a cloud of witnesses but a cloudy witness. The Sun of Justice, the Teacher of Truth, the Word made Flesh has never ceased to shine in the darkness for those who heeded His light, His voice, His Real Presence. He comes to chase away the shadows of ignorance and error. He does not compromise with them but dispels them for our salvation." That's as good as his predecessor, Leo XIII!

Father: Surely the most surprising part of the Bull was his rehabilitation of Archbishop Lefebvre, whom he called "a stalwart witness to the perennial Deposit of Faith in times of great confusion and dismay" and "a dedicated shepherd who, though sometimes confused and mistaken about the way forward (as were all who cared for the *depositum fidei* in opposition to the neo-modernists), displayed constancy in adhering to the Faith once delivered to the saints. He lived heroically the words carved on his tombstone: *tradidi quod et accepi*. In this way, Divine Providence was able to use his zeal to safeguard precious elements of the Church's heritage in a period marked by the wicked repudiation of that same heritage at the hands of the very ones responsible for preserving it."

Brother: Finally, a pope who speaks the truth, the whole truth, and nothing but the truth!

Father: Indeed! And the Church, as if with new wind in her sails, is finally having an effect again on popular culture. Did you hear about that musical *My Feria Lady*?

Brother: I did, though Broadway has never been my cup of tea. Speaking of which, apparently there's a progressive rock band called *Ad Disorientem*. Not my cup of tea either, but still, it shows that the people who said Latin are dead are now the ones who are dead.

Father: The old fighting spirit is definitely back in play. I have found a great deal of edification in that weekly column of the American Catholic journal... what's it called?

Brother: You mean *The Triumphalist*?

Father: Yes, that one. The column is called "Evolutionary Dead-ends," by Elabinna Iningub—a clever pen-name, that. He speaks very wittily about the once-fashionable ideas of the liturgists in the days before most priests had abandoned the Boomer Rite and returned to the old Mass...

Brother: ...in spite of the attempts of both Francises to prevent it!

Father: No doubt. But you can't stifle the Holy Spirit. Anyway, in Iningub's latest column, there's this priceless line: "As was often seen in the older generation of liturgists, Msgr Irwin showed a pardonable naïveté in thinking that the reforms called for by Vatican II were a good idea—and, even sillier, that they were responsibly implemented by the crew of drunken sailors who staffed the H.M.S. Consilium."

Brother: What I wonder is why it took so long for people to see this kind of thing, which now seems patently obvious.

Father: It's hard for scales to fall from the eyes. You know, all that überhyperpapalism that the Servant of God Father John Hunwicke used to talk about. But having two successive heretics in the chair of Peter was enough to deal the death blow to that fiction, not to mention the imperfect Council of Lateran VI, which declared the second deposed by Christ and replaced him with Leo XIV.

Brother: Who would ever have dreamed of living in such times as these? Seeing the depths to which the papacy can fall, and the heights to which it can rise!

Father: Forget not the word of the Psalmist: "My times are in Thy hand," and "I will bless the Lord at *all* times, his praise shall be ever in my mouth."[1]

Brother: But getting back to Iningub's remark, didn't you love what our guest Father Thistledown said at recreation the other day? "I only eat organic, and I want my Mass to be organic, too. Conventional agriculture is full of chemicals that build up in the body, and it's no different in the Mystical Body."

Father: Spot on target. And then we somehow got onto the topic of why the whispered parts of the liturgy are the most powerful, for the priest and the congregation alike.

Brother: Father Blendheim said: "Clara Voce is overrated. She's brash, even a bit of a hussy."

Father: To which Brother Benjamin replied, not missing a beat: "Sotto Voce, on the other hand, is a rare beauty: understated, gentle, pensive, quietly persuasive, fascinating, mysterious."

---

1. Psalm 30:16; Psalm 33:1.

Brother: I find it a sheer joy to sing the Office these days, with my heart so full of thanksgiving. I have this verse running through my head from *lectio*: "The steadfast love of the Lord never ceases, his mercies never come to an end; they are new every morning; great is thy faithfulness."[2]

Father: Amen to that, Brother. He always has the last word.

2. Lamentations 3:22–23.

About the Author

Peter Kwasniewski holds a B.A. in Liberal Arts from Thomas Aquinas College in California and an M.A. and Ph.D. in Philosophy from The Catholic University of America in Washington, D.C. After teaching at the International Theological Institute in Austria and for the Franciscan University of Steubenville's Austrian Program, he joined the founding team of Wyoming Catholic College in Lander, Wyoming, where he taught theology, philosophy, music, and art history, and directed the Choir and Schola. He now works as an independent scholar, writer, speaker, editor, consultant, and composer.

Dr Kwasniewski has published five books: *Wisdom's Apprentice* (CUA Press, 2007); *On Love and Charity* (CUA Press, 2008); *Sacred Choral Works* (Corpus Christi Watershed, 2014); *Resurgent in the Midst of Crisis: Sacred Liturgy, the Traditional Latin Mass, and Renewal in the Church* (Angelico Press, 2014); *Noble Beauty, Transcendent Holiness: Why the Modern Age Needs the Mass of Ages* (Angelico Press, 2017); and *A Reader in Catholic Social Teaching* (Cluny Media, 2017). *Resurgent in the Midst of Crisis* has also been published in Czech, Polish, German, and Portuguese, and will soon appear in Spanish and Belarusian.

Kwasniewski is a board member of The Aquinas Institute in Wisconsin, which is publishing the first complete Latin-English *Opera Omnia* of the Angelic Doctor; a Fellow of the Albertus Magnus Center for Scholastic Studies; and a Senior Fellow of the St Paul Center in Steubenville. He has published hundreds of articles on Thomistic thought, sacramental and liturgical theology, the history and aesthetics of music, and the social doctrine of the Church.